OWNER
SHIFT

OWNER
SHIFT

HOW GETTING SELFISH
GOT ME *UNSTUCK*

MIKE MALATESTA

OWNER SHIFT

How Getting Selfish Got Me Unstuck

ISBN   978-1-5445-2391-0   *Hardcover*

        978-1-5445-2389-7   *Paperback*

        978-1-5445-2390-3   *Ebook*

Photo by Mark Frohna

CONTENTS

FOREWORD

Do not let the title fool you. It is the selfless leader who does selfish things for the benefit of those they lead, the family they love, the communities they belong to, and the success of their organizations. To understand the motive of being selfish with the mindset that the result is for the benefit of others, is selfless leadership. It is an acceptance and understanding that it is not about self-centeredness, but working towards and discovering a better, humbler, servant-self that can have a positive impact on others. Taking the courageous steps to take accountability for the life you have created, to bring to fruition the best portion of yourself, and build a life of moral character is a service to those we love, lead, and engage with.

In *Owner Shift—How Getting Selfish Got Me Unstuck*, Mike validates a personal theme in my life: "You Teach Best in Life What You Want to Learn the Most." Through his story, Mike shares with you the lessons he learned from what he desired the most. It is a story of personal history, failure, success, and the teachings gained as a result. By having you join with him in entering the "Valley of Uncertainty," you will discover insight into how to overcome the many roadblocks to being personally honest with yourself and others. To project to the world one thing and live another (personal dishonesty) is a recipe for internal emotional erosion and unhappiness.

It is never easy to take ownership of our personal shortcomings, but it is essential for moving forward in life and releasing the mindset that holds us back from greater and more satisfying personal achievement. We all own our own business, and that business is "you." How is your business? Are you balanced, healthy, learning, improving, profitable, and at peace? What are your priorities? How do you personally and professionally define success? What are your personal core values? Are those priorities and definitions aligned with those core values? It is the act of sacrificing those values in the pursuit of misunderstood expectations that creates a lack of alignment in personal character. Without the losses, failures, sacrifices, and hurts in life, how do we truly understand what our character is made of?

Mike shares his losses, failures, sacrifices, and hurts, and the life lessons learned from them. We all falter, but it is how we deal with the fallout that determines our future and the ultimate framework of our character. You will observe Mike's vulnerability and humble clarity in sharing with you his "Four Fallacies," "Taking Inventory," and "The Five Words." To make the decision to sustain an existence in the "Valley of Uncertainty" is an excuse for not taking ownership of your past, present, and future. The "Valley" is a breeding ground for blaming, whining, finger pointing, and despair. Mike provides the tools to travel out of the Valley, whether it be big or small.

I believe what happens to you happens for you. We are not in control of each moment of our lives, but we are in control of how we react to those moments. I define courage as doing the uncomfortable, as that is what it takes to be a better you. Have the courage to enjoy the journey with Mike, and possibly do a bit of the uncomfortable.

Jay C. Rifenbary
Author, International Bestseller, *No Excuse!*
Vistage 2017 Speaker of the Year
International Speaker
President, Rifenbary Training & Development

INTRODUCTION

Overnight entrepreneurial success sells. It's a cool story to paint and fun to tell. All it took was five years of coding to deserve a huge payday. Pizza and Red Bull one week. Billion-dollar valuations the next. That's how you do it. Put that way, anyone would want to get in line to try.

But it's also rare. Exceptionally so. Rare like a great white thunderstorm.

Or Kim Kardashian.

I don't have a rare story to share, but I do have a real one. All too real. And all too common, unfortunately. My story is the reality of the kind of overnight success that most entrepreneurs experience. The kind that takes a hell of a long time. If you make it in the first place.

Mine is a story about an entrepreneur who started a company with big dreams and few fears. A delusional optimist who came out of the gate full of excitement. Hungry. Deeply committed to doing well. Then the losses came. Losing people, purpose, and pride started to wear on me. My entire perspective changed, and my optimism dulled. I fell into a valley of small dreams and overwhelming fear.

What did I get for a decade of having a pager clipped to my underwear while I slept?

Not an invitation to the three-comma club. That never came.

Instead, I rewarded myself with a ticket into what I've come to call the Valley of Uncertainty. It's where my entrepreneurial dreams and I went for treatment. Maybe to die. A place where I felt entitled to a better story than the one I'd authored and owned. Wishing I could erase who I was and become someone else. Someone better. Equipped with all the right stuff. I was no longer the delusional optimist. I was just delusional.

That's the club I joined. Nobody gets in line for it—not intentionally, at least. Whether it takes a couple years or decades, everyone inside the club is there because they've hit their lowest point. Their story is more grizzle than sizzle. So, they quit. Move on from whatever dream they had, depressed by whatever, or whomever, they see around them.

I think too many entrepreneurs stop or quit before they become what they could be. It happens every day. They bow out before their future really belongs to them. I know because I could have been one of them. I should have been. There are lots of reasons to quit, or at least to think about quitting. I bet I thought about all of them.

It's too hard. I need more life balance. I was better off when I was small. It's not fair.

Whine. Whine. And more whine. I did my share. To myself, at least. Otherwise, I was quiet about it. Tried to keep it hidden. It wasn't that I wanted to quit. I wanted the opposite. It was just my way of giving in to a problem that I couldn't figure out.

But entrepreneurs owe it to themselves to keep going. There are ways to get past the frustration and disillusionment. To figure it out. To go big.

That's really what we're in this for. To go as big as we can. That's what I believe. Not for the sake of being big and not for the money. But for the impact that a going-big attitude brings.

Going big is good for us. It keeps us fresh and curious. Fuels our search for answers. Frees up time. Keeps us in the right environment, surrounded by people we can learn from, who offer new examples of what's possible. We need to go beyond the people from whom we've already learned all there is to learn—like ourselves—and things we've done a thousand times over. Those things get boring, and being bored is the first step into the Valley of Uncertainty. We have to avoid that trap and focus on what we do best. Keep a positive mind. Concentrate on the process. Walk past limiting beliefs. Forget about fallacies. Ditch our perfect problems. Accept the truth and do something about it.

I wrote this book for the entrepreneurs who have big dreams that may be fading. Maybe the vision you started with is fuzzier with every passing day. You may feel like hitting the brakes because the light has turned yellow. Maybe you look successful. Everyone keeps congratulating you about whatever it is you've got going on. You probably accept the compliment, but in your own mind, you know the truth.

Inside, you feel surrounded by walls. Some of which you constructed. You spend each day facing walls too high to climb over and too deep to burrow under. You're stuck.

The walls are imagined, of course—like most things that keep us trapped. They're nothing more than a construct of the grind. The by-product of years of deep frustration. Of being lonely for too long. Thoughts about peaking too early start to swirl. Uncertainty reigns. Analysis paralysis is the game you're used to playing with yourself.

Every story is different and the same. Different circumstances and players. Same struggle and options. I know because I've been there. Inside those walls. In that Uncertainty Valley. Full of big, ephemeral ideas but no plan for how to turn them into reality. Questioning whether I had what it took—the energy, knowledge, pedigree, or resilience.

You can name just about any aspect of life as an entrepreneur, and I'm positive I had questions and doubts about it. Ones I couldn't answer for a long time. I became convinced that quitting was the best option. Second only to getting small again. If either had been doable options, I wouldn't be writing this today. Luckily, I had no option but to move forward. The bank wanted its money back, and our team's livings depended on the company continuing—on me continuing. I had to figure it out.

Without realizing it, I'd become my own worst enemy. I was the obstacle. The biggest thing in my way. Where I was and what I was feeling was exactly as I had planned it. Perfect orchestration, you might say. I was blaming what I'd been—the architect of the building. I was deeply complicit in creating the grind that I simultaneously hated. I expected things to get easier when I'd built them to be hard. I festered in a stale reality. Each new day brought no new knowledge or challenges. I was goal-less. A living example of Einstein's insanity definition—doing the same thing over and over and expecting a different result.

I owed it to myself to find a way out. To get help. Take a new risk on myself. Discover a way to deconstruct the walls. Create a map that would guide my hike out of the Valley.

The way out, the way to keep getting bigger, was right in front of me the whole time. Funny. I was missing it because I was in a virtual reality world that I'd designed. Wearing those stupid goggles that make you think that what you see is what is real. Forgetting that I could take them off. To truly see for the first time in years.

I'm no guru, and I'm not going to tell you what to do. I certainly won't tell you what's right or wrong. Or how many millions I've made. There's no secret formula in this book. I hate crap like that.

I'm simply an entrepreneur with a story to tell. A journey to drive you through. The one that got me off to a great start before it veered and took me off track to a place where I rotted for a while. Where I wasted so much time expecting what wasn't yet mine.

Until my messenger met me for breakfast early one morning. And told me about a different track. One that went a new way: up. To a future I could make my own. A future that I could build (with a lot of help) because I believed in it completely.

Come on. Let's put this thing in gear and take a ride together.

PART I

DREAM

1

THE SEED

An entrepreneurial seed landed on me in the summer of 1969, when I was four. It came from across the street and seeped into my senses over many days in the afternoon sun.

It happened on the curb in front of my house. I sat next to the 2110 my dad painted on the concrete curb in a simple, thick, black font to indicate our address. I was here for one reason: trucks. I loved them, from the real ones on the road to the toys I played with in my room. I wanted to be around them all the time to take in their ambience. When I wasn't drawing pictures of them, I was imagining what it would be like to drive them, just like Dad did.

OWNER SHIFT

Our house was on a one-way and oddly zoned street. Residential on one side, commercial on the other. My grandparents' house shared a wall with ours. My mom grew up there. The two houses were mirror images of one another, except that Grandpop and Grandmom's front porch was screened in. In Havertown, we called that kind of house a twin.

The Rouse construction company was directly across the street. Its building was two stories with a red brick façade. Their office faced the street. The shop was in the back. The yard was a mix of construction materials, everything from concrete to asphalt and hard-packed stone. The owner had a reserved spot out front where he parked his Mercedes on the days he was actually in the office.

On many afternoons in the summer, I sat on the curb by the numbers. Leaning a little forward so that my knees touched my chest, I waited for the Rouse guys to return to the yard with their trucks.

Because of the way the parking yard was oriented, the trucks had to enter the street against the one-way to access it. There was no other way to do it. The men maneuvered their trucks in the street directly in front of me. They'd tug the leather strap that hung from the headliner by the windshield to toot the truck's air horn. I was startled the first time I heard that. Before long, I asked for it. Flashing me a smile and a thumbs up, the guys shifted their transmissions into reverse and backed up into their parking position inside the yard.

Diesel engine noise and black exhaust smoke filled the air. Dust blew off the trucks and up from the street when their air tanks dumped, and into the wind when they moved like they were Pigpen from the Peanuts cartoon. I loved being in the middle of all the dump trucks and lowboy trailers carrying bulldozers and excavators on their beds. How cool! The experience was way better than my toys. The rigs were parked so closely together that the drivers had to shuffle sideways in between them. They looked like kids playing a game.

It was probably dangerous for a four-year-old to have a front-seat view of this action, but no one ever told me not to. For me, it was like being in my own little adult world. I wondered if one day I could do what they could do, what my dad did.

The drivers seemed to appreciate my audience. Usually, one or two of them rewarded me with a small gift. I might get a quarter from their pocket or a leftover Tastykake from their steel lunch box. Butch would share things from his lunch box with me many years later, when we became partners. The guys offered me advice too. Be a good kid. Do what my parents say. Work hard and stay out of trouble. I'd giggle and promise them I would.

I wondered what it took to have a company of your own, with a red brick office and a yard full of Mack trucks with your name painted on the side like our address stencil.

R-O-U-S-E. Was that something that just dropped into someone's lap? Why didn't my parents have that?

I probably asked my parents and grandparents about it, but I don't remember what they told me, if anything. I don't think that the term entrepreneur was used much in those days. They probably told me what it meant to be a businessman, or a boss. Or maybe they told me to go play with my friends or wash up for dinner because I was being annoying.

The truth is that they could have told me anything because I had no idea what a business even was. To me, it was just trucks and cars, noise and smoke, Tastykakes and quarters. And men who looked like they had a hard job.

At night, I would look out my window at the construction yard. It was locked up and quiet, like everything was asleep and resting up for the next day. In reality, things were buzzing to life. That entrepreneurial seed was coming to life. It may have stayed dormant for a long time—so long that I almost forgot about it. But it was always there, growing slowly, craving the right nutrients just below the surface, until the day a farmer came along who knew just what to do with it.

BIG-BOY
TRANSMISSIONS

Seventeen years later, I opened the door that said OFFICE and went inside. The room was small and grimy. It obviously hadn't been cleaned in a while. The block walls were painted white, and a single chair sat in one of the corners facing a single security camera hung in another. A clipboard of employment applications was on a counter in front of a one-way mirror. Typed instructions hung on the wall next to a phone. They told you to pick it up and dial seven when your application was filled out.

OWNER SHIFT

The office belonged to Ace Service Company, a trash hauling company on Delaware Avenue in South Philadelphia. Across the street from the river. New Jersey on its other side.

A tall and abandoned brick warehouse was adjacent to the north. Its windows were missing. The word "ROBIDEAU" was painted in block letters near the top of the building—a couple decades ago. More recently, painted graffiti tagged the lower levels of the building in stylish and bright colors. A strip club was next door. Some of the drivers took in the views there after work. And a few before, it was rumored. It's prime real estate now, but in 1986, it was a section of town no one wanted to be in for long.

I was in Ace's office because I didn't want to drive the Folsum Fence Company truck like I did last summer. My best friend, Tim, pulled some strings with his brother who ran the place to get me the job. I spent the summer delivering fence supplies to installers in the tri-state area. Chain-link rolls, galvanized metal poles, custom-fabricated gates, and barbed wire. I loved the driving but hated the deliveries. Everything had sharp edges and I had to unload at most stops by hand. A fresh tetanus shot was a requirement. I lost my share of blood doing that job.

During my junior year, I decided to set my sights higher for next summer's job. I wanted to drive a bigger truck and lose less blood. Trash trucks had gotten my attention. I passed a ton of them on the New Jersey Turnpike driving to and from my Folsum deliveries. They were bigger and cooler than my single-axle Brigadier flatbed. Over spring break, I stopped by five or six local trash companies to fill out an application. Most said I was too young for their insurance. One looked terrifying, with old trash-truck carcasses littered in the front yard, so I drove away without applying.

Ace was a bit of a hike from my house, but they had an ad for drivers in the *Inquirer's* help-wanted section. A woman told me to come fill out an application when I called. Maybe they were more desperate, or their insurance more lenient.

When I finished the application, I dialed seven, as instructed. The one-way mirror window slid open. A woman extended her arm with an open hand.

"Application and driver's license," she said, without looking at me.

I handed her both. She told me to take a seat and slid the mirror window closed.

The phone rang a few minutes later. I picked it up like I would at home.

"Hello?"

There was a man on the other end. He told me to go outside and meet a guy named Art for a road test. As I hung up, the woman slid open the mirror window and gave me back my license without a word.

A garbage truck idled in the street. A guy was standing by it waiting for me. He wore a uniform and a bothered look. I was clearly an interruption.

"Art?" I asked.

"Yeah," he said. He opened the passenger door and climbed up and into the truck. He'd left the driver's door open. I took that as my cue to get in, too.

He gave me instructions.

"Go up to the corner. Take a left. Go to the dead end. Turn around and drive back here."

I stared at the truck's dashboard and gulped. Trying to familiarize myself because I wasn't expecting a road test. It was way more cluttered with gauges and dials than my Folsum truck. It had eight speeds instead of five. A big-boy transmission.

There was a diagram on the shifter handle in the shape of an H with two numbers next to each of the vertical lines. I knew that meant there was a low side and a high one. I was trying to figure things out and reminding myself to breathe. I glanced at Art. He gave me a look that said, "Let's get going." I bit the bullet, put the truck into first gear and eased out the clutch. It began to move and didn't stall. Whew!

I drove through the course like Art told me to do. A couple of times the truck bucked like it wasn't sure whether to go or stop. That happens when you go too slow in the wrong gear. When I finished, I pulled the knob for the parking brake and wondered what Art was thinking. He kept that to himself.

"Someone will call you," was all I got.

I must have done well enough because I got the job. It paid $7.50 an hour to start. Eight dollars if I made it longer than two weeks. Two dollars more than I was making at the fence company. I felt like a big deal because I was going to be driving a "real" truck, like my dad and like the Rouse guys from when I was a kid.

I delivered and picked up large roll-off and lugger dumpsters to and from construction sites. The trucks were complicated and strong. Hoists and cylinders did the heavy lifting. Jockeying trucks like these took a lot of small back-and-forth maneuvering. You'd be surprised how much you can sweat doing a series of subtle movements in a huge truck during the summer. At least, you'd be surprised by how much I did.

It took most of the summer for me to get comfortable with what I was doing. The streets in downtown Philadelphia were narrow and crowded. They make you nervous in a car. Many streets were one-way, which complicated things further. Driving and dumping in a landfill was tricky, too. You run over a lot of trash. Avoiding mattresses was something they drilled into my head. Their springs wrap around the truck's axles and can stop the truck in its tracks. Nobody liked lying in a bed of trash underneath the truck to cut them loose.

Truth be told, Ace should have fired me that summer. I cost them a lot of money in mistakes and accidents. My creative destruction made a lot of extra work for Art, who turned out to be the company's maintenance manager. The twisted frame on the truck I nearly tipped over was a shitload of work to fix. Scary, too, for me, because the truck's cab was five feet in the air when it was all over. A couple of guys I didn't know helped me climb back down to earth.

There was the time I couldn't stop and damaged the front end by running it into a car that was stopped at a red light. It bounced forward like a heavy ball before I rolled into it again. I felt helpless and out of control. Then there was the freshly built block wall that I eased the dumpster into, and then through, due to a miscalculation when I was setting it down. That's most of it. The other companies that told me I was too young were probably right.

I would have fired me had the shoe been on the other foot. I think I was spared because I was young, polite, and showed up on time. No one at Ace wanted to fire the "kid," which had become my nickname.

Despite my sometimes-deficient driving, I loved the job and the trash business. At least the little I knew about it as summer help. I felt like a big deal. In control of something powerful. I had a skill that none of my friends had. Plus, it filled my bank account more than most summer jobs. Even when I had to start at 4:00 a.m., I was excited. I was working with adults at a real job. Maybe I wasn't the greatest driver yet, but then again, maybe there was something more to this experience than just the driving.

Shorty was my dispatcher. He ran the yard and yelled at everyone. He started at the bottom, picking up trash from curbs all over the city. He was a soldier of sorts. The guy we relied on to make everything happen. He maximized profit, kept the customers happy, and the drivers in line.

At the transfer station, we dumped the boxes we picked up from the streets into a compactor. Shorty ran that, too. He packed the loads we dumped into special boxes that we would haul to the landfill as our first load every morning. He was good at that, too.

His goal was to pack these boxes so tightly that the trucks could hardly pick them up. We got charged for dumping by the box size, not by the weight. Arbitrage. Not only were the boxes larger than their stencil said they were, but they were also heavy as hell. The arbitrage, aided by some deception, fell squarely to the company's bottom line.

My landfill loads were almost always more than 10,000 pounds over what the truck could legally weigh. When you raised the hoist up to dump them, sometimes nothing would come out. Friction fighting gravity and winning. That's what happened to me the time I tipped the truck over. Top-heavy plus unstable ground and a dash of driver inexperience resulted in physics taking over. Down went the hoist and the box.

Shorty also liked me a lot. Sometimes, he'd invite me into his control room. A twenty-five-square-foot wooden box with a phone, his trash compactor controls, and a window air conditioner. We'd shoot the shit or wait for a new pick-up order to come from the office. Before the summer ended, I asked Shorty to help me. Would he ask Ace's owner if he'd be willing to meet with me? I wanted some career advice. A path that I could follow. To lead me to where he was.

He got the OK, and I walked over to the office to meet Bill. I knew who he was, but we'd never met. His son-in-law was the only person from the office whom I'd met. Sometimes he would walk over to Shorty's control room. We got introduced one of those times. Bill's Mercedes coupe was parked in its reserved spot. His license plate was personalized; it might have been the first time I'd seen that. "Ace," was all it said.

I told Bill that I appreciated the opportunity and everything I learned so far at his company. I said the experience made me think about getting into the waste business as a career. That got his attention. Patient and gracious, he gave me advice that I took immediately. He told me that Ace was a family business. They needed more drivers, not more college degrees. If I wanted to get into the business, I should look at getting hired by one of the "big guys," he said. He suggested I try sales or a management training program.

"They've got needs and resources. They'd want someone like you."

He walked me to the door and wished me luck.

Sales? I didn't see that. It took all I could muster to have the courage to ask for the meeting with Bill. Not sure how that could work. But management, that was a future I could imagine as possible.

My fraternity brothers were all about becoming lawyers and doctors. Staying in school to get another degree. That wasn't for me. I wanted to study work and be done with school. I knew

I wanted to make money with trucks. I'd already dropped out once. Second semester, freshman year, when I thought that a job at the parish cemetery was my real calling. I figured I was fine as long as I could buy Girbaud jeans and a color TV. Brother Richard set me straight on that, so back to college I went. Now that I could get out legitimately with an English degree to fall back on, there was no other path I wanted to consider.

I followed Bill's advice. I had a friend type my resume and spent my final spring semester applying to the big guys. Waste Management and Browning-Ferris Industries. I got nowhere with Waste, but I got an interview with BFI. After a couple rounds, I got an offer I was happy to accept.

THE
FALLING STAR

I drove to Detroit two weeks after graduation to start my career. Bill's advice had paid off. I was about to be a newly minted management trainee for a trash company that was publicly traded. I would be working there for six months, maybe a year, they told me. Then I'd go somewhere else, to a place that was not yet known.

I was anxious to get started, but the drive from home to there was long. I had lots of time to think. I imagined what I was heading toward and missed what I was leaving behind—family, buddies, and my girlfriend. I cried a few times along the way— once in Youngstown and again near Toledo. Both were border crossings. I don't know why. Maybe it was just being on the road by myself and lonely. Heading west when all I had was east. I wondered if I'd find my forty acres there. It's easy to let your thoughts get the best of you when all you have in front of you is road.

When I got there, nobody knew what to do with a management trainee. I was expecting a plan, but there wasn't even a script. I felt like a foreigner, an alien from another place. I told myself that's okay. I'm flexible. You can put me in a strange place, and I'll adapt. Like I did with the eight-speed transmission on the road test with Art. Just put me somewhere, and I'll take it from there.

I spent the next thirteen months bouncing around different divisions. Working at field operations, mostly. On islands governed by corporate but rarely visited. I learned a lot, but I was also off the radar. I picked up trash on the streets of East Detroit and St. Clair Shores. I dumped garbage trucks into a hopper and squeezed the trash into giant semi-trailers that were chained to a huge, hydraulic ram in a transfer station like Shorty did at Ace, only on steroids. I drove these compacted trash loads to the landfill, without incident, as far as I recall. I also rode with drivers. Sometimes to learn and others to find out why one was taking too long to finish his route.

My first apartment choice was a big mistake. It was in the basement of a house owned by a woman in a wheelchair who stayed up all night watching TV with the volume at full blast. The washer and dryer were down there with me. Her family used them whenever they felt like it, like it was a common area. It reminded me of my fraternity bedroom, loud and lacking privacy. Always open for business. I felt like I was on alert all the time. No jerking off or lying around in my underwear. Being flexible was one thing, but this was too unpredictable.

A month there was all I could take. I had to get out or up to ground level at least. I found a room for rent in a ranch house that a guy named Liam owned. He dressed well but never showered, at least while I lived there. The handicapped woman yelled at me when I broke the lease. I felt bad. Obligations mattered to me. I liked finishing what I started. But I told myself that this was different.

Five years and four moves later, I was the youngest district manager in the company. The corporate path was working for me. I had an office in Milwaukee on a second-floor mezzanine. Through a huge window, I could see what was happening in the shop below. Our yard was filled with a fleet of trucks every night.

My boss called me in the morning on St. Patrick's Day. He wanted to pop up from Chicago that afternoon for a visit. Bob was round with rough edges. He had mutton-chop sideburns and a hoarse smoker's voice. His walk was a bit of a waddle, like a knee or hip might be bad. I respected him. He'd owned a large street-sweeping business in Indiana that our company had acquired a few years before. He had a house in Hawaii and lived there part of the year.

Our company was the second-largest trash business in the world. It grew by buying and consolidating a bunch of entrepreneurially run garbage companies. Many of these companies did other stuff besides picking up trash. Things like pumping septic tanks, sweeping streets, and putting portable toilets at construction sites and festivals.

Someone higher up than any of us had decided that these business lines were being neglected because picking up trash and dumping it into a landfill was what made the company tick. To change perceptions and create more value out of these operations, they were consolidated into a new, separate division called Special Services.

There was nothing special about them. These businesses were orphans, really. Parentless; in need of a good family. I didn't volunteer to become a special-services foster parent. I was happy with trash. It's where I wanted to be.

But I also had a rule to say yes to every opportunity. So, when a special services recruiter called me about one, that's what I said. Yes. Sight unseen.

That yes led me to a double-wide trailer leveled by cinder blocks in the middle of a Christmas tree farm in Pennsylvania. The ex-owner and his mom lived in an old farmhouse a hundred yards to the west. An inventory of portable toilets was organized to the east. There were hundreds of them, molded plastic creations, yellow on the top and puke green everywhere else. Each with its own "A Potty on the Spot" sticker on the door with a phone number.

Cute brand. Special indeed.

Bob's request for a meeting that afternoon was unusual, but I wasn't surprised. I had a feeling it might be coming.

A few weeks before, the office I was working in right before I moved to Milwaukee was raided by the FBI. My buddy Kevin called me after the raid and told me that the shit was hitting the fan. He took my place when I moved to Milwaukee. Worry was in his voice. Probably fear, too. The FBI is no joke. Not that I knew. Kevin repeated something we often told one another. That all we were doing was taking advantage of gray areas. Legal loopholes. I didn't know what to make of his call or what I could do about it. I felt bad for him. That had to be scary. I was worried, too, but carried on as if nothing happened. It was an easy decision. The only option, really.

Less than a week after Kevin's call, I was meeting with a private investigator at a diner near my office. He'd been hired by the company to get to the bottom of the situation. To find out whether there was anything to all this. He asked me what I knew, and I told him. He was a good listener, very understanding. I was convinced that this must all be a misunderstanding caused by crossed wires or fuzzy math. He said he'd get back to me, but I never heard from him again.

Bob showed up that St. Patrick's Day afternoon instead. He hadn't come alone. His right-hand man was there too, a witness to the impending execution. Ron was the smooth edges to Bob's rough ones. He had a corporate look, like a Wharton man. They didn't want to fire me. At least they said as much. The order came from higher up and they were obligated. But they didn't hem and haw about it either. They got right to the point, like pros. It was a good example of how to do that kind of thing right.

I wasn't the only one, either. Bob told me that Kevin and a few other guys on his team received an identical message and the same fate earlier in the day. It was a housecleaning exercise. Pure and simple. The damage may be done, but at least the damagers were now neutralized. Disassociated and sidelined.

Ron opened the office door. It was his sign for me to go. I was able to take my empty briefcase. What was in it had to be left behind. It would either be company property or evidence at some point down the road. A box with my personal stuff was left by the door to my apartment a few days later.

As I walked down the stairs, Butch was heating up a tank with a torch in his shop. Whacking it with a five-pound sledgehammer. I'd miss that guy. We didn't know one another well—hardly, really. The one thing I did know was that he was the hardest working guy I'd ever come across. Harder working than Shorty, and me, too. A haze of smoke was all around him while he worked, peppering him with sparks and metal-to-metal noise. I said goodbye but didn't stop. I don't know if he even saw me because he was busy, and I had tears in my eyes.

I left the office and didn't know what to do with myself. I couldn't go home. It was the middle of the afternoon. Only losers were home in the middle of the afternoon. A bar was an option. It seemed like a good place to think or commiserate. I could have a few beers, maybe a shot or two and forget for a while. It was St. Patrick's Day, after all. There would be no judgment. But I wasn't the kind to head off to a bar by myself, even on St. Patrick's Day.

I needed some time to think about what happened. I needed to figure out how I was going to talk about what happened. It would be easy to tell a stranger that the company and I had simply decided to go our separate ways. Creative differences or whatever. But that wouldn't fly with my wife. It wouldn't be fair, either. I hadn't told her about my call with Kevin or the meeting with the private investigator because I was hoping I wouldn't have to. I thought I would be able to skate right past that. That it would work itself out. In a way, I guess it did, just not the way I had been hoping it would.

I drove to the gym and spent most of my time sitting on machines. Doing nothing but being anxious. I was sure that everyone around me could tell that I'd just been fired. I could sense that they were feeling sorry and embarrassed for me, and about me.

That morning I'd been a rising star, and by the afternoon I'd been unmasked as a failure and a fraud. I was easily dispensable as worthless or troublesome. And now, I was projecting that image to the world. For sure, at least, to the ten people at the gym in the middle of the afternoon. My whole world, at the moment. Like I was carrying a S-H-A-M-E sign on my shoulders.

I got home before Jamy and sat on the couch in the dark. I practiced what I might say to her. Our dog Samantha listened, unenthusiastically. I heard the door open and started crying tears of self-pity and shame. Embarrassment, too.

I told her enough about what happened to satisfy myself. It wasn't everything. I mentioned that the guys I'd worked with at my last job got caught doing some things wrong. The company looked into it and decided to clean house. Every manager, present and past, had to go. Including me. I was a victim of a broad mandate. A collateral casualty. Wrapped up in their fuck-up.

She asked me the obvious question. Did I do something wrong?

I knew I probably did, but I told her no anyway. It just seemed easier—safer. I was still processing the whole thing and it wasn't making sense. I rationalized that wrong was too broad. Subject to interpretation. The whole thing was still very gray for me.

I left out a lot of details that I should have included. The incriminating ones, especially. I kept the stories of the FBI and the private investigator to myself. I left out the ripped-up dump tickets and doctored samples, too. Dilution is the solution. How the system came to be designed.

I also thought I could fix this. I thought it would all be better soon. A bump in the road you can only see in the rearview mirror. No point in making her anxious about something that will eventually go away.

DON THE DICK

The next day I needed something to do. It had been a while since I needed that in the middle of the week. Jamy had to go to work, and I was jealous. She mentioned the library.

The library?

"They have newspapers there. You can look for a job or just read. Take your mind off things. Chill. Think. I'll see you later when I get home."

She was so great.

I hadn't been to a library since college, and it wouldn't have occurred to me to go there, or even think about it.

I found it hard to think about anything for long once I got there. I was still replaying what happened yesterday in my mind. Like it was on a loop and maybe not even real. A dream or a movie. There were moments of distraction. The librarian shushing a kid that was reading too loudly with her mom. The guy who sat in the chair right next to me when there were lots of other empty ones he could have chosen. Inevitably, though, I'd end up back in that loop.

By Friday, I had my routine at the library. I felt like a regular even though I never talked to anyone. It was all head nods, half smiles, and eye contact. The kind of interactions that you have with people you recognize but don't know. The place was our bond. We may not have had anything else in common.

The only internet at the library in 1992 was the newspapers. They were the closest thing we had to real-time information. At best, that meant all updates were at least twenty hours old. When you don't know anything else, you accept real time as being whatever it is.

The newspapers occupied a special section in the library that bestowed upon them a certain royalty. There were a bunch of them. We had the two local papers, the *Wall Street Journal*, the *New York Times*, and the *Financial Times of London*.

They weren't tossed on a table or strewn about the place like you'd see in a coffee shop or on the subway. Instead, each paper was slid onto a wooden rod that looked like a fancy pool que. The rod had slits in the end that fileted the paper into its respective sections. When placed horizontally in the rack that held them, the papers draped toward the floor. Like laundry drying on a line. The pink pages of the *Financial Times* looked like whites that had been washed with colors.

The fancy rod made a twenty-five-cent paper seem important. Its reader regal. I felt employed even though I was looking for a job.

As each new day ticked by, I was feeling more and more desperate for a job. I'd called my old company's CEO to try to explain what I was still convinced was just a misunderstanding. I tried to beg for my job back. I figured he was my best shot, as I knew him from my interview when I first got hired as a management trainee. When he was a regional VP. I couldn't get past his secretary. I wrote him a letter, too, thinking that could work. The company ended up using all that against me down the road.

On Monday morning, I saw a job that looked perfect for me. It was in my industry and local. I wrote down the information and took it with me because tearing it out of the paper would have gotten me banned. I knew how to follow the rules most of the time.

I typed my cover letter and mailed it with my resume to the PO Box in the ad. A few days later, I got a call at home from Jim because that was the only phone that I had.

We met on Saturday afternoon at an industrial site adjacent to the sewage treatment plant. I had to turn around because I'd missed the entrance to his place at first. There wasn't a sign, just a locked gate—until Jim showed up to open it.

I wore my suit. Jim was wearing jeans and a leather jacket. His company logo embroidered above his heart. This was the "corporate-trained kid met his entrepreneur" moment.

I wasn't expecting it to be waterfront property. Lake Michigan was to the east. It was so big that if you didn't know any better, you'd think it was an ocean.

The place had been a chemical plant for decades. There were buildings scattered here and there, all with original uses long since expired. Some of the buildings were dilapidated and crumbling, like a bombing squadron had practiced on them. Others looked decent. Spared in the raid. Rocks and dirt had been piled here and there. As if a cleanup had been started and stopped.

Jim's dad died from a heart attack when he was nineteen. The business was his inheritance. He choked up when he told me about it. He was obviously still hurting. Jim was an open book. He told me a lot of things that afternoon. Married with two young kids. He said he could be kind of a hot head, which was why he thought he needed someone like me. He also mentioned, at some point, that he collected Mafia memorabilia.

"Random and cool," I thought. Jim was easy to like.

I mostly lied to Jim about why I was there. I know that's a terrible way to begin a new relationship. I didn't tell him that I'd been fired because getting comfortable admitting that would take me years. It's still hard. I told him that I was looking for a new opportunity because I had a difference of opinion with my old company (somewhat true) and decided (very untrue) to see what other opportunities I could find.

Jim's business had grown a bunch since he took it over. He was struggling to keep up with everything. He told me that he had good people that he could count on but no one who could run the business when he wasn't around. Things just seemed to happen all the time. Fires constantly needing to be put out. He was tired and frustrated. Vacillating between optimism and pessimism. He felt like he was just grinding it out, scattered, like his yard. He was unsure about where to turn.

Jim made me an offer before the interview was over. He told me that he'd have to swallow hard to pay me what I was asking. It was the same amount that he paid himself, he said. I think he may have been the one lying then.

I told him I'd have to think about it. That was another lie, but it seemed like the right move—a mask to cover my desperation. The job was exactly what I needed. His offer made me feel normal again, for the first time in weeks. Sayonara library. I've got shit to do again.

I made a mistake taking the job. That was clear before the end of the first week.

Part of it was the work environment. It didn't scream status. A couple of weeks before, I'd been a divisional vice president at a Fortune 500 company with a mezzanine office. Now, I was working out of a job trailer supported by concrete blocks. I felt like I was back on the Potty on the Spot Christmas Tree Farm, where all the trouble started. This trailer was in the parking lot of the wastewater treatment plant just up the street from Jim's office. The bathroom was a porta-potty or the Super America up the street.

The other part was that I had a chip on my shoulder. I hadn't stopped feeling sorry for myself about being fired. I thought I was owed something. I had an air of snobbery. I wasn't yet willing to accept that my world was very different than it had been. I continued to conduct myself as if I didn't get that memo.

I tried to talk myself out of what I was telling me. No problem. I can do this. I need to do this. What would I do if I wasn't doing this? It kept me showing up, despite the pit in my stomach that I soothed with Skittles and Diet Cokes that I picked up during my convenience store bathroom breaks.

It also turned out that Jim wasn't around much. He left me with the people he already had in place. I guess he expected them to teach me the ropes.

I didn't manage anything because the people Jim had in place didn't accept me—especially Don. They were never told that they had to. Besides the people, the job wasn't a challenge. Instead of making a difference for Jim, I was loading tanker trucks with sewage sludge. Pumped from a rubber-lined lagoon that looked like a giant pool of chocolate milkshake that was frothy on the top. Its life started as shit, but time and digestion transformed it into fertilizer. It had a new label and purpose: to be spread on farm fields far away.

Don was Jim's real number two. He'd been a complete dick to me from day one. He welcomed me by letting me know that he called the shots around here. He moved his face real close to mine and told me that if I didn't like it, I could fuck off.

Nobody had ever told me to fuck off before.

I tried to stand up for myself. I tried to convince Don that I wasn't a threat to him or anyone else. I just wanted to help. My pitch was similar to the one that the private investigator gave me before I got fired. Only Don didn't buy it like I had.

"I don't need your help, asshole."

Well, that didn't work. What a dick.

I knew that this wasn't going to work, but I was afraid to quit. Three weeks isn't long enough to make that kind of determination. Quitting now would be giving up too early. Plus, I'd be making no money. I'd be unemployed again. All things I didn't want to do or be.

The final straw made the decision inevitable. One morning, Don had emptied the filing cabinets onto the floor of the trailer and the parking lot. It was a mess. He told me to pick up the papers. Knowing life would be easier if we could get along, I did, even chasing after some as they moved around in the wind. Don stood in the doorway watching. A command-and-control look spread across his face, that then transitioned to a shit-eating grin. I pushed past him and put the papers all back on the desk.

Then I called Jim to quit. He wanted to see me first and came to the trailer. In the meantime, Don drove off to hide from Jim. He asked me to give him some time to talk to Don. He said he could fix things. That seemed unlikely. I was young but I knew that dicks like Don weren't easy to fix.

Here I was again. Unemployed and feeling lost in the middle of the day. A second gut punch. A two-time loser in rapid succession. The library in my future again. Thirty days later, I got a different message from a real Dick. I realized soon after that Don the Dick had done me a big favor. It wasn't his intention, obviously, but that just sweetened it for me.

5

MY FARMER

Butch lived in a small bungalow on Milwaukee's south side. His real name was Sylvester, but no one called him that. Not even his mom. I only knew that because I'd signed his paycheck. He was married to Dianne. They had four daughters. Julie was the oldest. She was already married and living in Cleveland. Nicole was the youngest, still in grade school.

I was at Butch's house in response to his message. It came to me through a real Dick. That was his name. Dick ran the portable toilet division where I had worked before Bob fired me, and where he and Butch still did. He had called me on Butch's behalf to tell me that if I was interested in starting a business, Butch would like to be involved.

The message was a surprise, completely out of the blue. We'd worked together before, but I didn't feel like I had that kind of bond with anyone. Definitely not with Butch.

When I moved to Milwaukee, I was convinced that the Pennsylvania work ethic was the best there was. But that didn't last long. Butch changed my mind. In the fifteen months that I'd worked with him, he proved to be the hardest-working person I'd ever met. Outside of that, I didn't know much more about him.

I knocked on his front door around seven. Butch was finishing his microwave-reheated dinner. I hadn't seen him since he was banging on that tank in the shop the afternoon that Bob and Ron fired me. His kids were upstairs. Dianne was doing the dishes.

He finished eating and took me outside to see his garage. He was proud of it because he built it by hand. His work clothes were in a pile by the back door. Dianne made him dump them there because they usually smelled like diesel fuel or worse: the perfume of truck. She'd get them later when she was ready to do the wash.

He'd also built a general store in the basement. It was miniature, but much like the one from the *Little House on the Prairie* or the lobby of a Cracker Barrel restaurant, where they sell all the knick-knacky stuff.

The store's attention to detail was striking. It was like a diorama at a museum, stocked with inventory that he and Dianne had collected over time from who knows where. Each item displayed carefully—complete with price tags, as if they were for sale. An antique cash register was on the counter by the door, ready to make a transaction final.

We sat back at the kitchen table, cans of Miller High Life in front of us. I learned about Butch. That he grew up on a vegetable farm in Oak Creek, just south of the airport. That being a farmer was all he'd ever wanted to be. High school was nothing more than an interruption. He graduated and met Dianne there, but all his effort was put to farming. While most kids were playing sports after school, Butch was helping his dad farm. When they were going to parties and school dances, Butch was fixing the equipment. Staying up late wasn't an option for him, because getting up early was a necessity.

He worked a night job at a factory to make ends meet. It wasn't enough. The farm went under anyway, squeezed by its small size and unpredictable weather. Costs always exceeded revenue—a familiar story for family farms. Devastating, but life goes on, was how he explained it to me. He drained his can and went to the fridge for two more.

Butch's family got to keep their house, thankfully. Gordie DeRosa bought most of the remaining acreage. He was not a farmer.

Gordie transformed the fields into a landfill for foundry sand waste. Butch went to work for him as a truck driver, mechanic, and landfill grader. Day after day, Gordie's guys were in and out of the molten metal-casting companies that were everywhere around Milwaukee at the time. They retrieved large metal boxes full of sand-casting remains that were thrown away after the sewer lid, engine block, or other part had formed and cooled inside of them. Each afternoon, Butch bulldozed and smoothed out the foundry sand piles that he and the other drivers had dumped that day.

Gordie treated Butch well. Better than he treated his own sons. They didn't have Butch's skills or his brain. His farmer's flexibility was not in their arsenal. He liked working for Gordie because he depended on him and treated him like a partner. They'd go to the Indy 500 race each year to hang out and have beers together. He thought that working with Gordie would be the last job he'd ever have or need.

Butch grabbed two more beers and told me that it didn't turn out that way because Gordie decided to sell the business. It was a smart move for him, Butch admitted. BFI bought it. A few years later, I ended up at Gordie's old shop. In the office on the mezzanine. Above the maintenance bay where Butch spent most of his time.

Gordie didn't stay on after the sale. He wintered in Florida. A lot of the time he spent around Butch evaporated, slowly, but noticeably, like the level of a pond during a drought. Everything that Butch thought his future would be was changing before his eyes.

He told me that before I came along, things were going to hell, that there was no management, and no one cared anymore about the work. At least not like he cared about the work. All anyone cared about was the credit.

It was getting late. The beer was having its effect, maybe not on Butch, but on me for sure. I had a ride home to think about—a future too. We walked to the front door. Then to my car. His kids were asleep by now. It was a school night.

"I'll be forty-one next month," he said, looking me in the eye. "I'm tired of starting over and getting nowhere. You care about things, people. Getting stuff done. I can tell. I asked you to come here tonight because I wanted you to know that. I don't know what happened between you and the company, and I don't care. I know that I want to work with you. Be involved in something you are doing. Whatever it is. Think about that. Please. I have money to invest. I'm ready."

My eyes began to water. It had been a couple of months since I felt good about myself for more than a few minutes at a time. I forgot what it felt like to think I had any value. Here was this guy I barely knew before tonight telling me that he wanted to hitch his wagon to mine. To make something together. Form a partnership. Break out on our own.

The drive home was crowded. Alcohol, thoughts, and traffic competed for my attention. I was trying to figure out what Butch saw in me that Don the Dick hadn't. I'd been wallowing around in shit for months, trying to figure out why what happened to me happened. Mostly, I was just wasting time. Instead of thinking about how I could use its energy. Its restorative properties. The growth nutrients. The positive rather than the negative.

At the library the next day, I started doodling pictures of trucks on pieces of scrap paper the librarian left on every table. I did it without thinking, the way I had in my grade school notebooks and on the grocery-bag book covers my mom made growing up. Expressing the thoughts that started when I was four and the entrepreneurial seed was first planted in me while I sat on the curb by the address stencil, blown away by the business across the street, by the trucks and their diesel exhaust, the smoke, and the smell. I thought about the reserved parking spot cuddling the fancy car.

Was that seed still inside of me? Lying dormant all these years? Waiting to be germinated? To be watered and fertilized by this farmer whom I barely knew?

It was time to find out.

FINDING FUEL

Confidence makes a difference. That's what Butch gave me. I was struggling with what to do, especially since the new job with Jim didn't last. Should I stay or should I go? Run away or hunker down? Take a risk or play it safe? The only reason I ever thought we might be able to be successful together is because he thought we could. His belief made it possible.

We talked about it, Jamy and I. We'd only celebrated one anniversary together, and I'd already moved her to a new place far away to play it safe and advance my career. Another step on my way to being the CEO. That plan worked out poorly. Went to hell in fifteen months, actually.

The safe rebound was even less successful. Lasted only thirty days. And now, I had my next "great" idea. To start a business with a guy she didn't know. With zero experience doing something like that between us. All it would take is risking all the money we had. She and her unemployed husband. Throwing whatever remained of safety to the wind.

She went along with the idea. Despite the obvious lack of a good reason.

"If it makes you happy, it makes me happy," she said, reminding me once again that I was lucky to have her.

A conversation at a kitchen table is only a catalyst. It gets you revved up, like a spark igniting fuel drives a piston, making the car speed up. It's excitement, not a business.

Butch and I committed to each other to give this a try. Now, we just needed to find the fuel. We needed money to get us going. We'd scrape together some and borrow the rest. It wouldn't be cheap. We'd buy a couple of trucks and start getting the word out. The plan was just to shoestring it and work for next to nothing.

There was a lot to do, and Butch needed to keep his job in the meantime for obvious reasons. Good thing that I had nothing going on except a part-time job delivering salt to vegetable canning plants to make a few dollars. Finding out what we needed to know would be on my shoulders. It took some work in those days without Google to search.

We went to an SBA seminar and took notes. They synced us up with a retired executive in their SCORE program. He helped us understand how to structure our plan correctly for a bank, with a checklist to follow. He stressed the importance of pro formas, a compelling story, collateral, and guarantees.

I wrote the business plan on a yellow legal pad. It was a product of my imagination—completely theoretical. A best guess, so to speak. Impossible to prove or disprove. It represented a story that I was willing to tell and had to believe. Words and numbers describing a future that couldn't be seen or touched.

Jamy typed it on her friend's computer because we didn't have one. We called our company Advanced Waste Services so that we would show up early in the yellow page listings. We wanted to show up after companies who called themselves some-thing silly, like AAA this or that, but before a lot of others. It was a simple wastewater trucking business. Easy for anyone to understand. We would pick up wastewater at factories and haul it to wastewater plants we'd find and negotiate with. The business would make money by charging customers for truck-ing and wastewater processing charges. We would mark up the processing charges a few cents per gallon and keep the spread. Legit arbitrage, much different than Ace's.

We needed $350,000 to get the company off the ground and keep it going until enough cash flow kicked in. That would get us two used tractor-trailer tanker units, cover rent, and pay Butch and me $30,000 salaries. It would also pay for business cards, letterhead, and a Gateway computer.

Butch and I had $100,000 of our own money to invest from 401(k) plans, CDs, and parents—in our case. Our SCORE counselor told us that banks liked "hard" assets like trucks, or any collateral that they could sell easily if things went sideways. That and our personal guarantees might be able to get a bank to lend us twice the equity we were putting in. I decided to push that to a request for two and a half times. I figured, why not?

Butch and I were willing to sign personal guarantees because we had to if we wanted to get a loan. We didn't know any better either. Neither of us had an appreciation for what signing those really meant. For the potential risk. We weren't concerned about the risk because we were so sure that our company would work. A duo of delusional optimists. It's what all entrepreneurs have to be, especially in the beginning.

He had a lot to lose if things went to shit. He was a grown-up with a house and a big family. I had less to lose, but all I had (and more) was going into this thing. There was nothing more to lose if it didn't work. All we needed now was a bank to lend us $250,000 and we'd be set.

I put on the suit I last wore months earlier to the interview with Jim and visited the banks that I'd cold called with our business plan in hand. We marked them like an art print, one of ten in this case, to make them seem special, like limited editions. Knowing what I know now, that probably made the bankers giggle. I had no idea what I was doing and no connections. I made appointments at the five branches closest to my apartment. Everyone was pleasant. Four said no or went silent. I didn't hear from them again until we got bigger. But it only takes one, and one of the banks eventually said yes, with two conditions.

The first condition was that they needed the SBA to guarantee the loan on top of our personal guarantee. Laurie was the branch manager. She told me that the bank could help with that. She said they do it all the time. It wouldn't be a problem.

The second condition was that we had to come up with more money: another $25,000 for the bank to make the loan. She apologized. The bank couldn't help us with that one.

This condition was a problem because we were tapped out. We had to go looking elsewhere.

Additional partners were never part of our thinking. There was no bullet point for that in our business plan. The bank's second condition changed that. To get this thing off the ground, we needed another partner.

OWNER SHIFT

I knew Chuck because he and I did business together before I got fired. He ran a waste business that his dad started. Took it over when his dad died young. He was the only person I could think of to ask for the $25,000 we needed.

Chuck was tall and had great hair. He was pleasant and happy, with a country-club feel. I'd caddied for guys like him at Merion when I was a kid. He drove a fancy car and had a sign in the parking lot reserving his spot. Just like Rouse and the owner at Ace.

His office smelled like natural gas simmering in a Crock-Pot. It gave the space a unique, anaerobic ambiance. If you didn't know what was happening in the back, you would have evacuated and called 911. Back there, his guys were evaporating water from oil brought there from the manufacturing plants in the area. It was a real mess. Smelly and slippery. When all the water was gone, the oil was burned at an asphalt plant that his brother-in-law owned.

We caught up with one another about what we'd been up to the past few months. The way you do with an acquaintance. Everything was going great. I was on pins and needles. He was calm and cool. Chuck worked at a wooden rolltop desk with a lot of cubbies to save stuff in. An antique barber's chair was bolted to the floor in the middle of the office, brown leather with a fancy footrest and completely out of place.

I pitched Chuck when I thought the time was right. He was polite and noncommittal. He only asked a few questions. I understood why. The optics weren't screaming that this would be a sure thing. I was an unproven kid and still kind of a stranger. I was only twenty-six at the time. Still freshly fired from the job I was doing when I met Chuck. Now I was starting a waste business with an unproven farmer he'd never met nor heard of, and I needed his help to do it.

He walked me to the door, gave me an "I'll think about it" before he let me out. Would he think about it, or did he just blow me off?

Later that week, he asked me to come back to Rockford for another meeting. A good sign. It was a ninety-minute drive. I used the time to anticipate what he might ask and what I might answer, writing my own screenplay for the meeting. As the miles clicked by, I was getting more and more nervous. This had to go well.

Larry and Randy were in Chuck's office. Two of his closest friends, he told me. Both had owned waste businesses and sold them successfully. They were their own little club of commonality. He trusted their judgment.

I sat in the barber's chair at Chuck's request. He explained why his friends were there. He wasn't interested in investing the whole $25,000 himself. He wanted a partner. If one of them wanted to split the amount with him, he'd go in. If not, he was out.

One new partner or two new partners; it wasn't a big deal. All I cared about was that one of them would say yes. I had no plan B if it was no.

I went into the pitch and tried to keep my arms still. I could feel that my armpits were sweating through my shirt. I didn't want to draw attention to that. Focus mattered. Flaws had to be minimized. They interrupted me with questions along the way, some that I'd scripted and others I hadn't. I left without a yes or no. Only a "we'll get back to you."

Chuck called me later that day and let me know that Larry was a yes. They were in. A YES! I was so excited that I forgot how terrible my clothes smelled from being in Chuck's office. Its odor clings to everything it meets. I'd become acquainted with a lot of odors that behaved similarly in subsequent years.

A HOARDER'S KINDNESS

Rick was a garbageman and a hoarder. The owner of Suds City Disposal. He lived with his mom and worked his routes alone. Butch was his one friend.

On Sundays after church, Butch would drive to Rick's shop to help him work on his trucks. This had been happening for years before Butch and I had decided to start a business together. When we got our loan approved, we didn't have a shop, an office, or a place to put things. Rick let us use his shop. We spent many hours there that November and December as we got ready to open our doors in January.

Butch was an "everything-in-its-place" kind of guy. The way he kept the general store in his basement was the way he kept his workplace and his tools. He was usually dirty but being neat was woven into his DNA.

Rick's DNA was different. His shop was packed to the gills with stuff. It was like a stuffed storage locker or one of those hoarder houses on the TV show. I'd never seen anything like it. There was a narrow aisleway from the front door. It led to the bathroom and to a tiny table with two chairs that served as the office and the break room. Sometimes the aisleway was so narrow that I had to turn sideways to make it through, just like the Rouse guys when they got out of their trucks. You'd be in trouble if the lights went out.

Butch never seemed to mind. He respected Rick's way and worked around it.

The shop had one large overhead door that allowed for a truck to be pulled in or out. Backing a truck into Rick's shop challenged my abilities. There was just enough room around the clutter to do it and get out of the cab.

While Rick kept lots of stuff, he was a man of few words. He only talked when he felt it was necessary. He reminded me of Marty, my friend Tim's other older brother. When I was a kid, he used silence and glare as weapons to intimidate me, and it worked.

Rick was pleasant but guarded. Not warm; careful, like words had betrayed him at some point in his past, and he didn't want it to happen to him again. It was obvious that he had a deep respect and love for Butch.

On the other hand, I was new to Rick. He hadn't made up his mind about me. I felt like I was a threat to him—someone who could hurt his friend. Like a neighboring tribesman who shows up with a smile on his face and a knife in his pocket. Amygdala stuff.

When I saw Rick years later at the funeral, I felt like he still hadn't made up his mind.

Having Rick's junk-packed shop to work in was a major blessing for us. I don't know how we would have gotten the pumps and hydraulics mounted on our first two trucks without it and his help.

Butch had built and banked years of goodwill and trust with Rick before he had to ask for a favor. I paid attention to that. If it wasn't for that, we would have been in a real bind. Trying to do this work in the alley behind Butch's house or in the drive-way outside my apartment would have made a great story but a lousy reality.

THE DAY OF FIRSTS

Butch and I took pictures of each other standing by our first tanker truck at the landfill. It was January 2, 1993. The camera was a disposable Kodak model that looked like a small cardboard box. We'd put fifty dollars of diesel fuel in the truck a few minutes earlier at the PDQ gas station. Filling it up would cost about $200, and we thought that being frugal was smart.

Getting ready for our first day in business had come down to the wire for various reasons. Not the plan, but sometimes plans don't work. We spent most of New Year's Day in Rick's shop finishing up our vacuum truck so that we'd be able to do the work we were committed to begin today.

The second of January was a day of many firsts for us. Besides the truck, it was also our first day in business and our first day as partners. We were about to make our first sale. Hauling our first load for our first customer. Cold and excitement were both in the air.

We'd been planning for these firsts since that day in May at Butch's kitchen table. But back then, it was all made up. Today, it was something we could see, feel, and smell.

You arrived at the former Delafield landfill by driving through an industrial park on the south side of the freeway. Past the Home Depot and the Area Rental store. Up a hill and past the custom hot rod shop where the asphalt road ended and a Do Not Enter sign was posted. After passing that, you downshifted to descend a steep, hard-packed stone hill before reaching the landfill boundary road. Then, you headed south to a turnaround spot that looked like a cul-de-sac. From there, you backed the tractor trailer up to a four-inch suction hose that was attached to a pipe that disappeared underground. You hooked that hose up to the tanker to load the leachate.

The landfill had been closed for years. Well-established grass now covered the large mound of garbage underneath. It looked like it could have been a park or a sledding hill for kids in the winter.

It was abandoned by its owner in the early eighties when the environmental laws changed. A lot of landfill owners did that then because staying in business no longer made sense to them. The changes would cost them millions of dollars that their business models and estate plans weren't built for.

The lawmakers thought that the new requirements would force everyone to clean up their operations. But a loophole in the law resulted in an unintended consequence. It gave the owners the ability to walk away from their dumps scot-free. Turns out that they did that in droves, making it someone else's problem.

For what had been the Delafield landfill, the state of Wisconsin was that someone. They were forced to accept the responsibilities that the owners avoided. One of those was the need to collect leachate from the site and haul it away to a treatment plant. To keep it from contaminating the groundwater in the area. Or at least, not contaminate it any more than the landfill already had.

We won the contract to haul the leachate back in October, before we were even a real business. We sent a low bid, and the state wasn't picky.

Leachate is a fancy name for the liquid that soaks through the garbage and collects underneath it all. Its slang name is garbage juice. If you've ever left your trashcan out in the rain, that nasty looking water you dump out of it is leachate.

A landfill like this one produces millions of gallons of leachate every year. Most of that comes from rain and snow. The water filters its way through the waste and ends up on the bottom. Along the way, it concentrates and usually ends up smelling like sulfur mixed with skunk. It can make you gag. It sticks to your clothes like a magnet. Like the burnt-oil smell in Chuck's office. People you walk past will look at you strangely once that happens.

For Butch and I, the landfill leachate and the other shitty-smelling stuff we'd end up dealing with for years to come would become our bread and butter. It all smelled like money to us.

A HOME

Butch and I said yes to every opportunity that came our way.
Even when we had no idea how to do what we were agreeing to.
Taking whatever came our way was what we were in business to
do. We weren't built to say no.

As soon as we had agreed to move forward with the business,
we thought that our partnership would work. But there was
still that little bit of unknown about whether it would. Until
something's real, it's not. After our first few months together,
the unknown was erased by the known. We complemented each
other perfectly. I couldn't do what he could. It made no sense to

try. We worked well when we were together and when we were apart. He could count on me, and I could count on him.

We also needed a home. I was looking for shop space so that we could move out of Rick's place. That's how I met Jerry, one of the biggest landlords in town. He wore a big smile and a hairpiece. The building we were at wasn't ideal. It was too small and not tall enough. The overhead door placement would make it difficult to get trucks in and out. I was convincing myself that it could work because we needed it to.

Before I could make what would have been a big mistake, Jerry bailed me out. I could tell he'd been doing his own thinking. He told me that he had the perfect spot for us.

I followed him and we ended up at a large warehouse. Its façade was cream city brick. Across the railroad tracks to the south were Harley Davidson and Miller Brewery. Both companies started from nothing in 1903. Jerry told me that it was fully leased except for a two-bay, 7,500-square-foot space in the front. You could drive through because it had overhead doors on both ends.

We walked through a steel door that was built into one of the overhead doors. It was on hinges so that it could be swung out of the way when the door was rolled up. The inside was dark and musty. The lights took a long time to come on, the way mercury vapors do. It was built in 1903 by a company that made trolley cars. Remnants of rail track were in both bays and on the outside. At some point they were filled in with concrete or asphalt. Probably when it became a bus depot in the 1950s, after they replaced the trolleys. The bathroom was in an adjacent bay. You had to slide a thick wooden door to the side with the help of its counterweight to get to it.

I showed the space to Butch, and he smiled. We were working in 450 square feet at Rick's, so it seemed massive. Too big, maybe. But cheap too, under our budget. It was our first introduction to more-is-always-better-than-less thinking.

Jerry leased it to us even though we had no credit history or track record. We closed the deal in his office upstairs. He joked that we shouldn't forget about him when we became big and famous. You could tell that it was something he was used to saying. The thing he told every new tenant. It still felt good and gave us a confidence boost.

When our second tanker rig arrived, we developed a good system that we used for the next five years to grow. Butch would be our primary driver, and I would be the additional support. We worked six days a week and sometimes seven. While he was driving, I would sell, pay the bills, and send out the invoices. When his driving plate was full, I would jump in the other truck to help. When I was driving nearly full time, we added a truck and hired another driver. I then went back to selling and became the support driver again.

We were frugal. We didn't want to waste money to heat the shop, so the winters were a bit of a bitch. We worked around it with a couple of propane space heaters that were on a cart we could roll around. We kept smaller propane tanks in the trucks because you needed them to thaw out the trailer's dump valve. It usually froze solid during the trip from a customer in Chicago back to the places in Wisconsin where we dumped. The tips of my fingers still tingle and hurt today in cold weather—the legacy of mild frostbite. A reminder of what those days were like.

We started without an end in mind. We didn't have time for that kind of introspection, not now. Not this early. Butch and I were yes men. Doers. Delusional optimists who saw no as a weakness, the property of lazy people. Strong backs were one of our biggest assets. Stronger than our smarts, Butch liked to say. Our only goal was to do what we had to do. To show up every day and grind. Work as hard as we needed to. And as long. Ask for orders. Take the opportunities that came our way.

We didn't have a mission statement or core values. Nothing posted on our walls except the minimum wage notice the government makes you put up. If you'd asked us what our purpose was, we would have looked at you like you were stupid. Our purpose was to survive. Duh. We were in this for the adventure. For the opportunity to change us. Make our own destiny. Chase freedom. Not to get rich or change the world. Those were the last things on our minds.

We were willing to do anything to make our business a success. Even dumb things. Things we should have thought twice about or said no to. To protect our health or preserve our integrity. We had simple aspirations and wore rose-colored glasses. We knew that we had a lot to learn and thought we were invincible at the same time. We had the attitude that every win made us more confident, and every mistake made us smarter.

PART II

GRIND

10

A TURN
IN THE HOLE

Car wash operators hate downtime and love extended weather forecasts. They try to do all their maintenance on shitty days like this one, when it's raining and might turn to snow. The days when no one gets their car washed.

This wasn't the kind of work we wanted to do. It was less than ideal. We took it because we needed the money and we never said no.

Car washes have systems to collect the dirt they remove. Usually, it's a pit or a tank underneath the washing line. If they didn't, the dirt would eventually clog the sewer pipes. After washing about 6,000 vehicles, that dirt collection system gets full, and the consolidated muck needs to be removed.

Thousands of gallons of muck were in the tank at this car wash. It was full to the top. We'd have to get inside it at some point. But that wouldn't happen until we removed enough muck to see the bottom. We needed to make a space for us to get in.

Butch got in the tank first. Then it was my turn to get in the hole. I had to insist. Otherwise, he would have stayed in there forever.

Normal people would wear a rain suit and a respirator for a job like this. It sucks getting soaked and there was no way to avoid it in there. The air has a funky smell to it, like natural gas. Like Chuck's office. There could be pockets of oxygen-poor air. It could kill you if you're not careful. The respirator protects you from that.

Rain suits and respirators cost money and, as you know, we were frugal. We knew we wouldn't melt. Our clothes would eventually dry. We were okay with being uncomfortable, with taking a risk. Especially if it saved us a couple of bucks. As for the air, the chances were slim, we figured. Worth the chance.

My tools were two five-gallon buckets, a short shovel, rubber gloves, my vacuum hose, and a flashlight. I sat on the bottom of one of the buckets. The second one had a rope tied around the handle. It was for the debris that wouldn't fit in the vacuum hose: pieces of license plate frames and antennas, rags, and soda cans. The rope went up through the hole in the top. Butch has a hand on the other end.

When the bucket was full, I would tug on the rope. Butch would pull it up, dump it, and rappel it back to me. This happened dozens of times. It's the most annoying part of the work because it takes forever. Like most people, car wash workers think that whatever you put in the sewer just disappears. It doesn't. It just hides for a while.

The flashlight was clinched between my knees. The tank was dark. Although it helped me see what the hell I was doing, it was hard to keep the flashlight steady while I worked with the rest of my tools. I was wishing that I had one of those lights that goes around your head, like a miner would wear.

Warmth was the one comfort that I had in the tank. It was cold outside where the truck was.

I was making progress. The suction from the truck was good. The muck was flying up the hose. There was evidence of tangible progress. I was amazed that washing thousands of cars can

make a mess like this. A few times, the suction would stop for no reason, like it needed to catch its breath. Some muck puked all over my boots from the hose like vomit when that happened.

The tank was completely full of muck when we started. Emptying it was a journey that lasted a few hours. Then it was done. I stood on my bucket and hoisted myself out of the tank. It felt rewarding, like getting a good grade on a test or winning a fight.

The tank was a mess earlier that day, a big problem for the car wash. Now, it was empty and clean. Ready to wash more cars. It was running better because of us. Because of the company we started. Maybe this was our purpose.

Experts tell us to find something that we're passionate about and do that. If you can accomplish that, they say, work is never work. Because you're doing something you'd do for free, the work gives you a ton of energy and makes your life meaningful.

OK. Maybe that works. Maybe it also holds us all back because we don't know, or can't decide, what we're passionate about. If we don't know, it can be easy to say no. To talk ourselves out of something that we haven't even tried. I know a lot of entrepreneurs. Real ones, not just the ones who talk about it from a stage or write about it in a book. None are passionate about *all* the work they do. Zero. And *Less Than Zero*—to borrow a Brett Easton Ellis book title—at the beginning, when things are just

getting off the ground. At that stage, you just don't have the time or the energy to focus on passion alone. There's work to be done, mouths to feed, bills to pay, customers to get and satisfy.

Here's how I think it really works. Five percent of us do what 95 percent of the rest won't. Not can't, won't.

Butch and I had no idea what we were doing as businessmen and entrepreneurs. We'd just entered that school. There was a lot of information that we needed to learn and lessons we would learn from applying what we were learning. Sucking up car-wash muck isn't a lot of fun. The working conditions aren't ideal. We weren't passionate about it, and we weren't above it either. It was just a job that we could do. Something we could say yes to. An invoice generator. A choice that the 5 percent take. A job that could increase the chances of our fledgling business surviving.

When survival is the goal and the things necessary to survive are within reach, you do them. At least that was our attitude. The question is, how long do you do them and how well do you apply the lessons you learn?

Passion would have to wait. Ideally, it would come. But it would be the by-product of our journey. A sweet spot that would reveal itself in between the pockets of muck—or in the light that filters into a tank through an open manway.

11

BROKEN COMPASS

I wrote the check, dropped it in the mail slot, and felt terrible. It would not have happened if I hadn't met Steve, but it wasn't his fault. It was mine.

When I wasn't driving or shoveling car-wash sludge, I was trying to get new business. One of my sales prospects made salad dressing. They washed down their production area several times a day and treated the water with a system in the back of the plant. Every two weeks they hauled away a load of sludge from that system.

Al was the plant manager, and he avoided my calls. I left messages with the receptionist but never heard back. I'd done my research. I knew that I could save Al a bunch of money on his sludge disposal. Why wouldn't he want that?

Steve called me out of the blue. I'd never heard of him or his company. He told me that Al asked him to call me and that he could make an introduction. That he'd been doing business with Al for a long time. We should meet, he said.

Steve's company recycled paper and cardboard. It was on a dead-end road with giant potholes caused by years of truck traffic going in and out. They were filled with water from last night's rain.

He drove a black Mercedes and wore sunglasses indoors like a celebrity. Slicked-back hair with cologne that arrived before him and stuck around after he was gone. He was happy and confident, always smiling like he had the world right where he wanted it to be.

When we got in his car, Steve opened his glove box. Inside was an envelope stuffed with cash. He showed it to me like he was a proud parent. On the way out, he weaved back and forth to avoid the potholes, like I'd done on my way in.

Al's plant was close by. Steve put the envelope in his coat pocket and brought it in with him. Al was a gracious host. He wore a suit that fit him perfectly. Pocket square and all. He spoke glowingly about Steve.

"Wow," I thought, "this Steve guy really knows how to build great customer relationships." I felt like I had no idea what I was doing. I was taking mental notes like I was in a sales training course. I missed seeing the cash change hands.

Al took us on a tour. The plant smelled like a salad bar on steroids. A giant French, balsamic and blue-cheese blend. In one area, ingredients were being mixed in stainless steel vats. In another, finished product was poured into giant cans and fiber drums with plastic liners. They shipped product to restaurants, hotels, and prisons across the country.

I got what I wanted from the meeting. Al told me to send him a proposal. Steve drove me back and acted like a mentor the whole way. He was happy for me, and I was grateful to him.

Al called me for the first time after he got the proposal. He wanted to meet to talk about it. We arranged a lunch meeting at a tapas place he liked. He had to tell me how to order because I didn't know what tapas were.

He told me that his family emigrated from Italy, how he started working on the shop floor and became the plant manager five years ago. When we were done eating, he pulled my proposal from his jacket pocket and unfolded it on the table.

"There's only one problem with your quote."

OWNER SHIFT

"What's that, Al?"

"It's too low."

Too low? I didn't understand and he saw that in my face.

He told me to send him a new quote and what it should say. He would switch his business to me. The only thing was that I had to charge him the same rate that he was paying already. He took out a small notebook from the breast pocket of his shirt and started writing.

He tore the paper from the notebook and gave it to me. On it was his son's address. His name was Daniel. He leaned closer and gave me instructions very matter-of-factly. As if there wasn't anything strange about it. I was to send his son a check for the difference between my first and second quote every month.

I thought about the envelope in Steve's glove compartment. This kind of ask was a first for me. Like tapas. I knew what I should do. You know what I should have done. It was a simple decision. Black and white. Only I could make it gray, and I did. I ignored my moral compass. After all, I'd been able to justify my way through gray areas before. Even though it's what got me fired before. I could make this seem like it was right. And if no one knew...what's the harm?

Maybe there's more to sales than being the best option.

The third time I dropped a check in the mail slot was the last time. The next time Al needed a pickup I made it myself and asked to see him when I was done loading.

He was very pleasant and made a good effort to talk me out of my decision.

"We're paying what we've always paid," he told me. "So no one is getting hurt here."

We both knew that wasn't true.

I told him that the only thing I could do was to charge him what I'd first quoted. It felt weird to say no because we were always saying yes. But it felt weirder to write the kickback check and put it in the mail. It gave me the same feeling that driving to work with Don the Dick gave me.

The first few years that I was working at BFI, when I was still a rising star, the CEO was Bill Ruckelshaus. I got to sit next to him for lunch at an annual company meeting in Houston. It was a "CEO spends some time with the up and comers" moment that someone had arranged. I didn't know Bill and this lunch didn't change that. But I "knew" him because his reputation preceded him. He was a strait-laced, heavy hitter. A Harvard Law School grad, Bill had been a congressman, a US attorney, the head of the EPA—twice—an army drill sergeant, and now a CEO. He was famous (or infamous) for resigning from President Nixon's cabinet rather than participating in what became the Watergate cover-up.

Bill had a thing for billboards, like Tim Ferriss does today. I only remember one thing that Bill said that day when he took the stage to address the group. It was a moral compass message. He said, "Don't do anything that you wouldn't be proud for your mother to read about on a billboard."

When Bill told us the billboard thing, I was already on my way to being fired from his company for things I was doing and would not want my mom, or anyone, to see on a billboard. I was blind to it though. I didn't see it. I'd let that sneak up on me.

Not this time. I remembered Bill when I was dropping those checks to Al's son in the mailbox. What I was doing with Al would make a bad billboard. My mom would be mortified, and I'll bet Al's mom would, too. My compass may have been broken, but there was still a chance that it could be fixed. I wanted to take that chance.

I figured that was the last time I'd ever hear from Al. That I was hauling our last load for him. I knew that this was the right thing, but I was scared, both about losing the business and getting caught.

I was surprised when we kept the business. For more than twenty years after. Al was let go at some point along the way. No one ever talked about why.

12

WHEEL SLIP

We were growing. Not saying no was working for us. The trucks were rolling. Our backs were holding up, muscling us out of many jams.

Two employees became four. Four became eight.

In two years, we needed more space. Jerry freed some up, and we moved across the courtyard into 25,000 square feet. I still worked from home mostly, but we added an office trailer in the shop, like the one I worked in with Don the Dick. It had a phone and a fax machine that printed on a roll of waxy paper.

We used it for team meetings and a place to warm up because we were still too frugal to turn the heat on.

Our business was working. Invoices went out. Checks came in. Bills and the bank got paid. We had a PO Box with a little window in it. It was exciting to peek in and see that it was full of envelopes with checks.

We were the first new competitor in a long time. The more established ones were satisfied with the way they did business. Even when their customers weren't. That disconnect was our opportunity. To be that something fresh and different. Even if it was only by a little.

I was driving less and working longer hours. My job was to keep it all going. Make things happen. Deliver what we promised. To callous our minds to no, the way David Goggins talked about in his book.

We made our first acquisition in 1994. Less than two years after we started. Buying a division of the company I'd been fired from, and that Larry still worked for. A division that I had run.

Larry found out about it. They didn't know he and I were partners and never asked. We didn't think that they'd sell it to us because I was involved; not a chance in hell, for reasons that'll soon be clear. We needed to get around that detail. Larry figured out how.

We set up a shell company and bought the assets for their book value under a new name with no clear affiliation. We called it Ental Environmental because one of Larry's buddies told him that ental meant "environment" in French. It didn't, but we decided to stick with it anyway because it sounded fancy.

We didn't have the money to close the deal. Chuck and Larry asked their friend Randy. Remember him? The one who passed on investing in the company's startup. This time was different. He lent us the money. It was a fascinating adventure. M&A with a hint of espionage. Larry playing the role of a double agent of sorts. I took notes and learned.

While we got it done, the rub was that we only got trucks and accounts. The drivers were union and they stayed behind to replace someone else with less seniority. It complicated things but was best for everyone. We had to replace them and fast because the sale came with a five-year contract to handle loads that had to be hauled right away. The contract could be worth millions over time, so we had to perform.

The acquisition changed things. Accelerated them. It wasn't part of our business plan. Kind of like partners; it just happened. I had to catch up to it. We all did. A bit chaotic isn't an overstatement. Disorienting, like a pilot trying to fly through a dense fog without instruments. It required a better business compass than the one I had. To be a companion to the moral one that Al had helped me find.

Some days it wasn't clear whether we were gaining traction and heading upward or spinning our wheels on a slippery slope. Those were reactionary days. For the six months after, I went back into the truck a lot because I told myself that it was what I needed to do, and it probably was. The acquisition looked easy on paper. It made perfect sense. We thought that getting the money would be the hardest part. When Randy agreed to loan us that, it made the rest of the deal look like a cakewalk. Instead, it was a shit show most of the time. It wasn't until we were able to expand our foundation to support the acquisition that it started to make sense.

Making this acquisition work (it would be the first of many) was another big turning point for me. Like meeting Butch around his kitchen table and finding a new home, thanks to Jerry. Making it work tested us. Some days, we regretted the decision. Butch and I were tired all the time. More than once, we jokingly asked ourselves how dumb we could be. But once we were supported by our expanded foundation, I forgot about how hard it had been. That quickly moved to ancient history in my mind. The experience made us stronger. It tested our mettle and our mettle won. Proof again that we were one of the 5 percent doing what the other 95 percent won't or can't. In my mind, I claimed victory and convinced myself that anything was possible. Acquisitions were now part of our business plan. There wasn't a high enough wall that our hard work wouldn't scale us over, or power us through. At least that's what I thought.

13

BILLY

Adding new drivers isn't easy. Adding them fast, like we needed to, is even harder. We were already stretched thin before the acquisition. Butch and I were driving ten or twelve hours a day. So were the other drivers we'd already added to our team. We used the weekends to catch up. For maintenance, billing, and whatever else was left on the pile, which was getting bigger with the new work from the acquisition.

Luckily, our help-wanted ad performed well. We added four experienced guys to our team.

One of them was Billy.

I was surprised to hear from him. He worked for Don the Dick too. I met him during that month a couple of years ago. We didn't keep in touch.

He told me he'd finally had enough. That he was tired of Don's bullshit. That all he wanted to do was drive. He needed to relax. Stay calm. Get his stomach back to normal.

Billy was a tiny man. Short and very thin. His pants never wanted to stay up. A belt was no help. He had long hair that was thin and wispy like mine. Gifted with bright eyes and an engaging smile that conveyed kindness with a hint of naughtiness. A lot of his teeth were missing. So many that it was uncomfortable to look at him if he wasn't wearing his dentures. In a way you wouldn't expect, that added to his charm.

Billy was genuine and unpolished. He was a get-what-you-see kind of guy, totally comfortable being himself. He was hardworking and fearless. He took no shit. Guys who thought he might because of his size found out the truth the hard way. He was a little like a cartoon character. Being around him made me happy.

Billy went wherever I told him to go and did whatever I asked. He started early and finished late. He said that he loved being home, but he stayed in his truck's sleeper bunk a lot. Even when he didn't need to. It kept his world small and manageable.

He tipped his tanker rig over one morning on the Eisenhower Expressway. A captain with the Chicago Fire Department let me know. At 9:37 a.m., my pager vibrated. I didn't recognize the number. That wasn't unusual because I gave my pager number to everyone. I called the number and the captain answered.

He was in a mood. You could tell that something had fucked up his morning. He told me that one of my trucks was laying on its side in the left lane between the Pulaksi and Kostner exits. That was clearly it. He had lots of questions. *What's in this thing* was the most pressing one.

My brain went into search mode, going through my schedule in my mind to figure out who it was.

It had to be Billy.

He was relieved that the material Billy was hauling wasn't hazardous because that would have ratcheted up the response another few levels. Still, he kept barking at me. Wanting to know how long it would take to get trucks there to pump off the tanker. Loaded as it was, it was too heavy for the wreckers to pick it up. The captain told me that he was evaluated based on clean-up time. He was serious. The faster he got wrecks like this cleaned up, the better he looked.

I asked him about Billy. All he knew was that the medics got him out of the truck and on the way to the hospital.

I headed to the scene. It would take a couple of hours. I was worried and anxious. Scared. Fearing the worst for Billy and the business. Would he be OK? Would we be in trouble? Would our insurance work? Could I handle it? Would I cry?

Butch was already emptying Billy's tanker when I got there. Scott was helping him. I'd freed up their schedules and sent them here. The tanker was on its side, like it was taking a nap. It blocked the highway's left lane and shoulder. Several additional lanes were blocked by cones, police cars, and fire trucks. The police forced the traffic to sneak by on the right shoulder. People were angry and late for work. They cursed at everyone.

The roadway was scraped up from the tanker's slide. It left a trail, like a slug does, for a hundred feet or maybe more. Two giant wrecker trucks were waiting for it to be emptied. Cables from each attached to yellow, nylon straps wrapped around the tanker's barrel.

Metro trains run back and forth from O'Hare Airport to downtown Chicago on tracks built between the Eisenhower's east and westbound lanes. They're protected by concrete barriers topped with chain link fencing, like you'd see at a racetrack.

In most truck rollovers, the tractor and trailer go over together and stay that way. From a bird's eye view, they look pretty much like they do when they're driving down the road. Billy's accident wasn't like most.

Ahead of where the tanker lay, a large portion of the fencing was mangled. That was where Billy's tractor climbed the barrier and left the road. It had come to rest on its left side, up against a storage shed. It wasn't on the tracks, so the trains were running as usual.

Its roof was collapsed. Its windows smashed. The wheels had become separated from the frame. They were up against the concrete wall. It was horrible to imagine the trip Billy took in it. Its passenger door was missing because that's where the medical team got him out.

Butch finished putting Billy's load onto his truck. Nothing spilled. The wrecker drivers worked their respective hydraulics and straps together and uprighted the tanker. They placed its tires gently back on earth. Then, it was on its way to an impound yard. The passenger side looked normal, like nothing happened. The other side looked like someone had taken a few smacks at it with a demolition ball.

Billy was in the Cook County Hospital ICU. He was alive, but I wasn't allowed to see him. The nurse said he was pretty banged up. They were doing everything they could.

She wasn't telling me anything I hadn't expected after seeing the driver's side of his tanker.

Billy's wife came to the hospital with her sister. It was our first time meeting. We waited together. He died later that day. Peacefully, they told us. He was unconscious when he came in and never woke up.

I knelt in front of Billy's casket a few days later. I didn't say a prayer. I just talked to him about how much I wanted him to still be here. How I wished that he was at home, watching TV with his wife, eating pie that she'd freshly baked. With ice cream. I knew that he loved doing that. He enjoyed his sweets, even at the expense of his teeth. I told him that I was sorry and that I felt responsible. And then I ran out of things to say.

What do you say in a situation like this? To Billy, or his wife? To their daughter? I was only twenty-seven. I hadn't had a close family member die, let alone someone who'd worked with me. I was lost. This wasn't part of the plan.

There was no finality to Billy's death.

We all wanted to believe that he'd been cut off by a late-for-work driver, that he'd taken evasive action, risking his life to save others. Like a fighter pilot with a missile on his ass. When his load shifted, the G-force took over and there was nothing he could do. We wanted to believe that Billy was a hero.

The police never found any evidence to confirm that belief. It was just as possible that he got distracted or fell asleep.

My closure was that I'd put him in a situation that caused him to crash and die. That his family held me responsible for his death, and that they were right.

I hadn't signed up for this. No one had. But I was in charge. This happened on my watch. It was my first tragedy. The first big punch in my entrepreneurial gut.

I couldn't change what happened to Billy, no matter how much I thought about it. And I did that a lot. Every time that I passed the freeway exit that would take me to the cemetery where he was buried. I got off the exit the first few times I drove near it after the funeral. It felt good, and right, to stop there and pay my respects. Before long, I'd just think about him when I saw the exit sign for Highway G. I'd smile and tear up at the same time. It wasn't a happy cry like when a woman gets an engagement ring. The smile was for him, and the tears were for me.

The Workers Compensation Fund cut a check to Billy's daughter for $100,000. That's what it paid for a life lost at work.

It sounded like a lot at the time, but I realize now that it was peanuts. I wonder how she and her mother got on with their lives without Billy.

What I didn't think much about was how what happened to Billy may have changed me. It shook my confidence for sure. I want to believe that I grew up some as a result of it. That I understood the weight of my responsibility better. The reality, though, was that I didn't think much about it. Not consciously, for sure. It was just another thing to push through. This tragedy wasn't about me. Making it so would have been selfish. I was a lot of things, but I was not selfish. There was too much else to do.

SHIT HITS FAN

Mike Wallace was a hard-nosed investigator on the TV show *Sixty Minutes.* He had a talent for making the people he interviewed feel uncomfortable. He brought up topics they didn't want to talk about. Things they knew about and avoided.

They got nervous, like Nixon with Watergate. Sweat on the upper lip and all that.

We were watching the show when the phone rang. It was September 11, 1994, around 6:30 on a Sunday night. The phone was on the wall in the kitchen. Larry Owens was on the other end of the line. He was an FBI agent and got right to the point.

He was investigating the company that I'd been fired from a few years ago. He said that he needed to talk to me in person, for an interview at his office in Philadelphia.

He was very polite, the way you can be when you're in total control. He was used to making requests that are hard to say no to. Backed up by the power to make it so. This was new territory to me. I wanted to change the subject because I didn't know what to do. I thought maybe I could get him to talk sports or something. I wondered what he knew. I was nervous and started sweating.

FBI? Was this real?

Maybe it was a prank. Something that my buddy Tim thought would be funny.

The only thing that I could think to do was to ask Agent Owens if I could talk to my lawyer and get back to him. He gave me his phone number and a week to do so.

The thing that began as a great opportunity for me on a Christmas tree farm back in 1990 was now turning into something much bigger than losing a job. That gray area thing that got me fired was starting to amount to something serious. A black-and-white thing, mostly black.

Agent Owens's call forced my hand in a couple of ways.

First, I had to come cleaner with my wife and my business partners. They knew some of the truth about why I had been fired. Just not the whole why. It's one thing to be married to, or partners with, a guy who'd been fired from a job. It's another to be either of those with a guy under FBI investigation. The change in circumstance was meaningful.

I justified it like this: we were operating in what I was told were gray areas. Taking advantage of legitimate loopholes. Doing things that everyone else was doing. What I thought was a good job. I was a low-level guy following instructions. I believed my bosses, and I worked hard to make them happy. If I knew it was wrong, I wouldn't have done it. I was just doing my job. I had justification after justification.

I left out the details about how we dumped loads we weren't supposed to. How we lied about what the loads were and where they came from. About our process for throwing away dump slips so that we wouldn't have to pay for those loads. How I knew about everything and played the game well. Each of those truths conflicted with the victim card I was playing. My story depended on everyone believing I got screwed by the company when I was fired and was about to get screwed again by the FBI.

I needed to find a lawyer. Chuck's lawyer was the only one I knew besides some of my fraternity brothers and Nuge from the neighborhood. Don helped us with the legal documents when Chuck and Larry invested. He couldn't help me because he didn't do criminal defense work.

Criminal?

Being contacted by the FBI meant that I was part of a criminal investigation. That part hadn't registered with me until Don mentioned it. I knew it was serious. But criminal? That's nuts. *All we did was operate in a few gray areas.*

Don knew a criminal defense lawyer and introduced me to Paul. He had a calming presence. It was almost fatherly. He talked with agent Owens and set up the interview. We walked through his initial thoughts together. The reality of the situation and the possible outcomes. It could be an uphill battle. The government's got the upper hand in these kinds of things. Power. Money. Deference in court. Not to mention the truth.

I felt scared but also like I was in good hands. Paul would work things out for me.

We flew to Philadelphia. Before my interview started, Paul met the prosecutor in a small conference room. I fidgeted in a nearby reception area chair. Their meeting was short, not more than five minutes.

Paul sat next to me and delivered the news. Calmly and in a whisper.

It wasn't what I wanted to hear. I would be charged with multiple felonies. It was inevitable. They didn't know when, and it might take a while. A lot has to happen between now and then.

They hadn't asked me a single question yet and my future was already determined.

15

BLACK AND WHITE

I dreamed that this meeting would be about setting things straight. I'd explain the innocence of gray areas and show them that I was a good guy. That all of this was much ado about nothing much at all. I'd leave with all of this behind me. Maybe they'd even say thank you for making sense of the mess and apologize for the inconvenience.

Instead, I felt like my life was over.

The bright side was that I no longer had any false hope. It wasn't bright at all. I was in deep shit, and everyone there that day knew it. Delusional optimism was put to bed. It was time to cooperate and come clean with everyone. My only hope was that the truth would set me free. Channeling John 8:32. No one else's fate mattered.

I spent the next few hours answering questions. They'd obviously done their homework. It felt like they were fact-checking me. Corroborating what they already knew. Confirming that I was honest—as honest as someone accused of being dishonest can be.

Despite the whirlwind the Philadelphia visit brought, the work still needed to be scheduled. Late in the afternoon, before Paul and I caught our flight back home, I put together tomorrow's schedule and called the guys. It was my daily ritual. The only ritual that felt normal to me that day.

I told Jamy that things went OK, that we made some progress. I didn't want her to worry. The whole truth wouldn't be helpful. I told myself that protecting her from the awfulness of the situation was the best way to proceed. I was also probably trying to protect her from my own awfulness. I didn't think that she would still want to be around me if she knew the truth. I knew the truth and didn't want to be around me.

Months passed and we didn't hear anything. Not a peep. Paul told me to just carry on with my life. Don't worry. Compartmentalize it.

Limbo is an uncomfortable place where uncertainty runs the show. Some days were normal. These were the ones where I was able to follow Paul's advice. Most weren't. More often, my thoughts vacillated between wishing it were a dream I'd wake up from and just getting it over with, like Martha Stewart did.

I could never be sure about who I was. I would be a criminal at some point down the road. It would be public then. Knowing that was like being able to see the shoe waiting to drop. But for now, it was private. Only a few people knew. The prosecutors and the people I used to work with—the ones who were now in trouble just like me—knew the real story. The few others that I told—Jamy, Butch, Larry, and Chuck—knew a portion of it. The portion that I convinced myself gave them a feel for the situation while preserving some of my integrity. I felt like I could deal with this and maybe even make it better on my own. Power through it like I had a lot of other things. Another "5 percent doing what 95 percent won't" opportunity that I could somehow come out of victorious. I didn't want to pull that S-H-A-M-E sign back out. Suppressing my emotions felt like a better move. There was no need to bother the people I respected most with the gory details of my past.

The choice to conceal the darker details felt right to me at the time. It aligned with who I was and what had worked for me. I was the private guy who kept his nose to the grindstone. Other people could rely on me and trust that I never needed extra help. Asking for help was a sign of weakness. I was embarrassed enough on my own for everyone. I didn't need to be felt sorry for. That would be selfish. There were other people in their lives who needed that more than I did.

There's a reason most people can't keep secrets. Hiding things takes a toll. On your mind, body, and relationships. While I convinced myself that keeping secrets made everyone's lives easier, the reality looked much different. The secrets ate away at me, a little bit every day. Instead of building confidence in myself or trust with my partners, they tore me down. I focused too much on what I was running away from, which stole focus from what we were trying to build for the future. I had a great team around me, but I left them all on the sidelines for months and months.

The long delay was intentional, right out of the prosecutor's playbook. Time is the best way to unravel a conspiracy. Pressure the lower-level people to cooperate. Be a pebble in their shoe that won't come out no matter how many times you take it off and shake it. Make them uncomfortable, only able to think about their personal preservation. Tell all you know and maybe we can get your sentence reduced. Make them sweat. See how high up this thing goes. Follow the path to the largest fish. Where the biggest headline waits. It's a proven game plan that works—with drug cartels, the mafia, and waste management companies.

The grand jury was part of their pressure plan for me. It was more casual than I imagined it would be. Not for me, but clearly for the jury. I was dressed nicely and scared to death. They were dressed like they were hanging around their house. Jeans and T-shirts, flip flops and sandals. Reading the paper and enjoying a morning cup of coffee. One woman was knitting a sweater. She smiled at me. Others had dozed off. Arms folded across their chests. Heads hung forward. Feet crossed. There was an abundance of boredom in the room.

I testified as a witness before the grand jury, which was strange. My job was to help the prosecution make its case against me, my old company, and some of my former colleagues. Weird. The government reimbursed my travel expenses and paid me forty bucks for my time. They treated me like I was truthful and legitimate. At the same time, they wanted the grand jury to indict me because I wasn't truthful or legitimate.

The indictment was unsealed in November 1996. Six years after I'd done anything it said I had. That part of my life was public now. It was a disturbing read. I came off like a criminal, which was its intention. According to the sentencing guidelines, I was facing up to eight years in prison, $500,000 in fines, and monstrous restitution.

I knew it was coming and had a good idea of what it would say. Still, I was surprised. I wished many times that the whole thing might just all go away. The indictment stabbed that wish through the heart. My secret and shame were no longer private matters. I entered the unknown territory of how to deal with their now-public nature.

I'd had plenty of time to better prepare for this day. To have solid answers and defend myself. The process had taken forever, after all. Plenty of opportunity to use the time wisely. But instead of answers, all I had were questions.

Would my wife stick by me?

What about our newborn daughter? What would having a criminal dad do to her?

How about my friends? Would they be understanding, supportive? Would it change the way they thought about me?

Would my business partners want to be associated with, and have their investment depend on a felon?

What would my employees think?

How about the regulators? I'd just lived up to the stereotype. Another guy in the waste business being accused of a bunch of crimes. Someone they'd have to keep their eyes on. Could they take the permits we relied on away?

How about our bank? Would they dissociate? Call in our notes? Protect their reputation?

And what about our customers? How would they take this news?

I could no longer operate as if nothing was happening because something was definitely happening now. I had to deal with questions and figure out answers.

I knew that most people would look at me differently. Even the ones who liked and trusted me the most, with whom I'd made a lot of goodwill deposits, like Butch had with Rick, the hoarder. Facts like this have a way of changing the way things are.

I met with my partners and offered to resign. I apologized for letting them down and took the appropriate responsibility. Falling on my sword was an offer that I had to make. Sure, this stuff had happened way before I met any of these guys, before we ever thought about starting a company together. But still. I couldn't expect people to compartmentalize that fact the way I could.

They declined my offer. Despite what they'd read and what I told them, they all thought that I was getting screwed. We were in this together, they said. What a relief. I didn't want to leave and had no idea what I would do if I did, or where life would take me. I don't think my partners ever realized the favor they did me that day. I would have been largely unemployable had they let me resign. My life would have been different for sure.

Still, some things had to change because optics are important.

Being the company president was one of those things. It's never smart business for the president of a company to be under indictment and maybe going to jail. Larry replaced me and I became the general manager. This helped us save face with our external stakeholders like the banks and the regulators. It also helped us get Larry more up to speed with how the business operated. Just in case I ended up having to go away for a while.

We had a company meeting to talk about what was happening and what it meant to everyone. It was a low point for me, but I kept it at a high level. This had nothing to do with our company or them. It was all about stuff from my past only.

If I had to guess, they were all curious to know more. I would have wanted to know more. They were probably reluctant or embarrassed to ask. It was kind of them to avoid further humiliating me. I was already drowning in it. There had to be talk around the water coolers, in the break rooms, and over the CB radios in the trucks. Whatever the chatter was, they kept it to themselves. No one ever asked me for a one-on-one. They only wanted to know what they needed to do.

My life under indictment went along much like it had before. It wasn't a national story, and the internet wasn't on everyone's devices. Social media wasn't a thing yet. Local news from Philadelphia didn't easily make it to the Midwest. I could pretty much hide in plain sight. Keep the situation manageable. If the same thing happened to me today, I'd probably be toast. I guess I caught a lucky break there.

After the indictment, the process took two more years. Like before, this was intentional—a way to keep the pot boiling. To give the guys who were thinking about fighting this thing and going to trial some time to rethink their strategy. They wanted the weight of everything to get to them.

During that time, things seemed normal on most days. I did my work, and the rest of our people did theirs. It never came up when we went out to dinner with friends. It was always on my mind, but I could sometimes put it aside and act as if I was the pre-indictment me, blissfully unaware.

I shouldn't have had any expectations of privacy, peace, or understanding. I didn't deserve empathy. It doesn't work that way for people under indictment. I knew that I had some explaining to do. That people we were working with—customers, suppliers, and regulators—had a right to ask about it. To cover their asses.

What happened?

How'd you get involved?

Have you changed your ways?

How would I know that?

Still, when the questions came, my initial reaction was always, "Fuck, not again." I didn't object to their scrutiny. It made clear sense to me. What I objected to was how I felt. New waves of shame hit every time a new line of questioning started. I felt horrible about myself. And sorry that people needed to scrutinize me. My parents didn't raise me for that to be necessary.

A competitor mailed copies of my indictment to our customers. They arrived in manilla envelopes with no return address. Anonymous, except that we knew where they came from. This caused requests for phone calls or meetings with me, understandably.

I dreaded and looked forward to every meeting like this. Dreaded because I knew I looked like a piece of crap on paper. Looked forward to because it was an opportunity to put the best of whatever foot I had forward. To be contrite and accept responsibility. Be genuine and humble. Embarrassed and honest. Worthy of a second chance.

I knew I couldn't talk myself out of the problem that I'd behaved my way into. I owned that. Expressing a victim mentality was a losing strategy.

Most of the people we met gave me a second chance. Some weren't concerned at all. "It's a non-issue," they'd say. Others lectured me and passed judgment. That didn't feel good, but it was their right.

We only lost a few accounts. Nothing major, fortunately. I was energized to make up for what I'd put them through. Convince them that they made the right decision to work with us. The first time and this time. I wanted to prove that a tiger can change its stripes.

But it was bigger than just that. I knew that getting myself into this mess was a dumbass move. Not the first dumbass move I'd made, but definitely the most consequential. It was who I was and who I wasn't at the same time. Simultaneously true and false. I hated how I felt about that and wished that I could change it. Make it go away or stuff it down a sewer like the car wash guys did with their trash. Hide it in a place where even I couldn't find it.

That was wishful and lazy thinking. Disingenuous, too. It was a continuation of my desire to take the easy way out. To make things gray and imagine them all away. Reality refuted that way of thinking. Tigers can't change their stripes, and neither could I. They were an indelible part of me. An undeniable truth. Unerasable, I realized.

While that truth was undeniable, it was only one truth about me. Another truth was that my stripes were just a part of me. An unfortunate and regrettable part, but still just a part. Was I willing to allow that part to define me? To make that part the thing I was always thinking about and always trying to hide from sight, hoping no one would open the sewer manway and find it? That seemed like a terrible strategy. Another dumbass move.

What if I just stopped making dumbass moves?

I needed to get to work on understanding and defining my whole. The calculation of my nature and character. To prove myself all over again. Make the whole of my stripes reflect the person I was and wanted to be. The person who people deserved me to be. The person who I deserved to be. One with stripes that you could trust and count on. Honest and hard-working stripes. Stripes you could believe in without question.

I had work to do.

16

LIBERTY

Paul and I flew back to Philadelphia early one February morning so I could be sentenced. We took a cab to the courthouse on Independence Mall, in the historic area of the city. There are still cobblestone side streets there from the 1700s. I'd driven past the courthouse many times the summer that I worked for Ace. When I convinced myself that the waste business would be a great career for me.

It was a nice day to walk around. Warm for winter. To mix in with the tourists and the people on their way to work, we bought soft pretzels and Diet Cokes from one of the vendors on the street.

Breakfast of champions. The Liberty Bell was on display in a building nearby. It was free to get into, so we stood in line for a ticket. I hoped that seeing it might bring me some good luck. Being that it's a symbol of freedom and independence.

We sat on a wall with a bunch of other people, waiting for our turn. I noticed Gary, my old boss, walking our way. I knew that I wasn't the only one being sentenced today but it surprised me to see him. He'd quit before the raid but got caught up in everything anyway. I hadn't seen him in eight years.

He was heavier than I remembered and a little bloated looking. He was smoking a cigarette like he wasn't comfortable with it. Held between two fingers by a tentative hand, like an amateur, but it was just his style. It was good to see him. Made it clear that I wasn't as alone as I'd thought all this time. Seeing him brought back memories. Of us shooting the shit in the shop when that was our den of equity. Back when he depended on me to make the work happen. Before we had to tell on each other to save our respective necks.

We shook hands and did a mini bro-hug. I knew that Gary had been divorced since this whole thing had started. I'd heard it was because he was having an affair and not because he was about to be a criminal. Either way, this wasn't the time to bring that up. We small-talked for a few minutes, like you would with an old friend or boss. He asked me when my time was. I told him 1:15. Soon.

"I got probation and a fine," he said with a sheepish smile. A mix of embarrassment and gratefulness. I told him that I was happy for him because I was. Then we didn't know what to say to one another.

"Well...good luck," he said, before walking away toward his future.

Paul and I looked at each other with optimism. What happened to Gary was encouraging for me.

I'd never been in a courtroom before. Jury duty hadn't found me yet. It was uncomfortable. I wasn't raised to be in a place like this, about to be sentenced by a judge for felonies that I committed. This was what the future looked like for the bad kids from my neighborhood. The ones who quit school, did drugs, or joined the Warlocks motorcycle gang. Not for me. I was a private school kid. The football captain. The college graduate and entrepreneur. Former rising corporate star.

On paper, I had no business being here. Except for the paper the indictment was on.

The bailiff called the court to order, and the judge made quick work of the hearing. He looked at me over the top of his reading glasses. I'd pleaded guilty two years ago, when I was first indicted, but he asked me if I wished to change my plea. Reminding me that it was my prerogative.

No, your honor.

He let the lawyers argue their respective sentencing wishes and whys. Paul argued for probation. The prosecutor for six months in prison and a fine. My cooperation reduced what I otherwise would have been facing. There's a whole formula to it that you can look up, if you're interested.

Then it was my turn to take responsibility and ask for leniency. Paul told me that this was important. He said hearing from me directly makes a difference to the judge. If there was ever a time to put my very best foot forward, this was it.

I gave the judge the best *I'm sorry* story of my life. Honest and emotional. I included plenty of regret. It was easy because I was sorry. I'd accepted what I'd done, and I was ready to pay the price and move on.

He thanked me for my comments and paused. Maybe for effect or maybe because he was changing his mind. I was pretty sure that he'd prepared for this moment and already knew the sentence that he'd hand down. If I were him, I would. Unless a defendant came across as a real asshole. That could change things, I supposed.

I was sweating like the time I was in Chuck's office asking for money. I was sure I sweated through my suit by this point.

He took off his glasses and looked straight at me. All of us were standing. Adhering to protocol. The judge said a lot about cheating and lying, damages and cooperation, and accepting responsibility. It was all a blur because I was only focused on the punishment. That was where my future was. A lot was riding on what the punishment was. I wanted to fast forward, like you do with a long proposal to get to the price at the end.

It finally came. Two years' probation. Two hundred hours of community service. A $3,000 fine. No prison time or restitution. The company had paid millions to satisfy that. Phew! Court dismissed.

We shook hands with the prosecutors and the FBI agents like we'd just done a business deal together. They wished me luck, and I believed them. We'd developed a codependency of sorts over the years that this thing took to wind its way to now. They needed me, and I was reliant on them. They always had the upper hand, of course. It was their job to do what they did. If I hadn't done what I'd done, they would never have been in my life in the first place.

And that was that. Paul was waiting for me in the lobby. It was almost eight years since I'd committed the crimes I was just sentenced for. That chapter of my life was closed.

17

NINE LIVES

The sun shone brightly in a brilliant blue sky. A perfect harvest day in October 2003. Warm without the sweat. The kind of day that made a farmer feel like he worked in paradise.

Butch was stuck inside working with the rest of the guys. They were in the middle of a project. Renovating what had been Chuck's oily wastewater treatment plant. The one that smelled badly and was attached to his office. Where I'd asked him and Larry for money nearly eleven years ago to the day.

We'd recently taken over its operation. The permit rules were changing, and the plant was out of compliance. It was also a slippery mess. The opposite of paradise. Oily slime coated every-thing. Upgrading the plant required a lot of tank and plumbing changes. Old stuff needed to be ripped out and new stuff put in. Sometimes the work took finesse. At others, brute force did the trick. Butch could always figure out what was most appropriate.

Before lunch, Butch cut the diameter of a tank we were scrap-ping in the unloading bay with an acetylene torch. It was too big to fit out the door, so he had to separate it into two pieces. A large letter C was written on its side with a paint pen. That meant it was empty and clean. His plan was to use the forklift and a chain to pull off the top piece first, take it outside to the scrap pile and come back for the bottom piece. That plan hit a snag. Although the tank was fully cut in half, the forklift couldn't budge the top section when Butch tugged at it.

Noticing that a pipe was sticking out the top of the tank, he figured it had to still be connected to the bottom. That had to be the problem. He got inside the tank through a hole on the side, close to the floor. The torch came with him so that he could cut the pipe and fix the problem. He was alone in there. Feeling reasonably safe because of the big C. The rest of the guys were in another part of the plant, unaware of what Butch was up to.

The fire alarm surprised everyone. Water started raining from the sprinkler heads. Butch was still inside the tank. Sitting on its floor. Knocked down by a flash of fire that burst from the pipe as his torch sliced into it. Wondering what was happening. Flames spewed from the top of the tank. Bouncing off the ceiling and draping themselves around its exterior. Like a campfire heating up water for coffee. The guys came running. Smoke filled the plant. They could hardly see. Or breathe.

Rico heard Butch crying out for help and went into hero mode. He looked into the hole that Butch had climbed through, but only saw darkness and smoke. Rico held his breath, closed his eyes, and reached inside. Like he was diving into unoxygenated waters. The direction of his arms guided blindly by Butch's faint calls for help. The other guys fought back the flames with fire extinguishers. Sweeping them back and forth until they were empty.

The tank's metal was hot, like the burner on a stove that someone forgot to turn off. Rico's skin singed with each contact. He felt Butch's arm and grabbed it. He pulled him toward and through the opening. Butch was disoriented, in shock probably. Assisting Rico's efforts with his innate survival instincts. They couldn't avoid touching the tank, and each were repeatedly burned. A few steps later and they were outside in the sun. Their clothes and bodies smoldering. The rest of the guys helped them take their clothes off and lie down on the grass to wait for the ambulance and the fire department.

Butch lost consciousness before help arrived.

Jeff told me about what happened after the ambulance had taken Butch and Rico to the hospital. He and Butch were partners on this project, like they had been on many. They shared a birthday and were perfect complements to one another. Always one-upping each other with humor, regardless of the shit they were up to their elbows in.

It was bad, he said. Rico would be OK, but he was worried and scared about Butch. You could hear it in his voice. Jeff made me concerned but not worried. Mostly because Butch was the toughest guy I knew. It might look bad, but I was sure he'd be fine. He'd be back to work in no time, just like he was the time he broke his collarbone.

I'd called Dianne to let her know what had happened and that I was on my way to get her. She played it calm and normal.

She and Butch built their dream house on ten acres in the country a few years earlier. It was a long ride to work, but he didn't care. Not quite a farm, but a big upgrade from their bungalow. There was a separate shop building for his tools and toys bigger than that whole house. Private and spacious. Evidence of the return on investment of our partnership.

By this time, Butch had replaced his Ford Ranger with a decked-out F-150 that had all the bells and whistles. Even a personalized license plate, YSIMBB. He was proud of the truth of its meaning: Your Shit is My Bread and Butter. No one could figure it out on their own. He liked that. It made him laugh.

Their driveway was a half-mile long and it came up on me quick. I missed it the first few times I'd been over. Equally spaced pine trees lined each side of it. Butch spent hours every night watering them to make sure that they took root properly. They got whatever they needed to thrive. He talked about admiring them in his old age. Typical Butch.

The garage attached to the house was open. I knocked on the mudroom door. No answer. I knocked harder. Still no answer. I opened the door and yelled her name. I heard hello from upstairs and walked into the kitchen. Her cats rubbed up against me. Making friends. Dianne gave me a hug. Remarkably calm still. I wasn't sure what to expect, but it wasn't that.

She'd talked to the emergency room doctors from the hospital. They couldn't treat him properly. He needed to go to a burn center and there wasn't one in Rockford. They were making arrangements to send him to St. Mary's in Milwaukee.

We had to wait for the doctor to call back to confirm that St. Mary's had room for Butch. Dianne asked if I wanted anything to eat. Just like she had every time Butch and I were sitting around the kitchen table at her old house.

She looked at her cell phone, like she was willing it to ring. "I've been preparing myself for this day for a long time. I mean, you know who we're dealing with here. I just never thought it would be a bad burn." She never said what she thought it would be.

Dianne knew that Butch was a risk-taker. Not in the dare-devil way. He wasn't jumping out of planes or doing flips on a motor-cycle. He just competed hard with himself. Like Tom Brady. He could be reckless too. He was no stranger to metal pieces in his eye, welding spark burns on his arms, and finger lacerations. Dianne was used to all that. He was a cat with nine lives.

The doctor called back with great news. A Flight-for-Life heli-copter would have Butch at St. Mary's in about an hour.

The burn center admitting station was on the sixth floor. Dianne called family on the way but no one else was there yet. It was just us. The floor nurse sat us down and explained what to expect. His burns were serious. Third degree over 70 percent of his body. There would be problems. Time was of the essence. They were experts. He was at the right place.

Dianne interrupted her, "Where is he now?"

The nurse checked and came back. "They say he'll be here around 7:00," she said.

"Seven? They told me 5:00 or 5:30. What's the delay?"

"I don't know. There could be lots of reasons. But he's in good hands. You can be sure about that."

"Keeping him hydrated is essential," she continued. "In situations like this, moisture tends to quickly evaporate from the body. The burns will cause a lot of swelling. We'll have to thinly slice his skin to relieve the pressure. It's not uncommon for lungs and kidneys to want to shut down."

She was preparing us to imagine more than we'd be ready to.

I felt more worried than I did before, but I still had faith. I reminded myself that Butch was very tough. That alone was good reason to be hopeful.

Dianne thanked the nurse. She was still calm. Very calm.

By eight, Butch and Dianne's family members had all arrived. The hospital set us all up in a private waiting room a few floors down. It had chairs and small couches for crashing. There was a table in the corner with magazines fanned out like a deck of cards.

Only Butch was missing. At this point, he was hours late from what we'd originally been told. They blamed the delay on unforeseen issues every time we asked. The nurses kept telling us that's all they knew.

We heard a helicopter just before nine. A few of us were given permission to go back up to the sixth floor to see him come in. There was a separate elevator to the helipad. Its doors opened with commotion.

They rolled the table carrying Butch past us, through a set of double doors, and we were not allowed to follow. He was wrapped in a silver blanket that looked like the material used to keep delivery food hot. We could only see his head. It was red and bloated. He was unconscious or sedated. Maybe both.

Later, the helicopter nurse knocked on the waiting room door. Her uniform was a blue jumpsuit. Like the one Tom Cruise wore in the *Top Gun* movie. She asked to speak with Dianne alone, but Dianne insisted she could say whatever she had to say to everyone.

"We ran into some trouble getting your husband here," she said.

The troubles had been mechanical, logistical, and procedural, like the troubles that led to Butch needing the helicopter in the first place.

The first helicopter sent to pick up Butch broke down. It was stuck on the hospital's roof. Her helicopter was dispatched to get him but of course it couldn't land on that hospital. He had to be moved by ambulance to another hospital that could land a helicopter. The move was complicated and time-consuming. In the confusion, Butch wasn't strapped to the gurney properly. When they rolled him from the ambulance to the hospital entrance, he slid off and onto the ground, hitting his head.

The nurse was in tears by now. As was everyone else. But not Dianne.

"Oh, honey I know," she said, holding the nurse's hands in hers. Trying to soothe her, like a mother would. "It's okay. Everyone makes mistakes."

18

LOST
IN THE VALLEY

It was hard to sleep that night. There was too much to process. Butch and Rico were in the hospital. We still didn't know how badly each of them was hurt. There was also the matter of a partially burned-up plant that couldn't process any wastewater until it was repaired. What would that interruption cost? How long would it take to get that back up and running? How would our team handle the news? Especially the ones who were there, who saw the entire day unfold. There was insurance, OSHA, and workman's compensation. What would happen to our record and our rates? What would all this cost and did we have enough money to handle it?

My wife and I got to see Butch the next day. We donned full-body protective suits because of the high infection risk. When I saw him, I thought they'd made a mistake, and put us in the wrong person's room. His face was bloated. He looked nothing like himself. Stewed red. Strained, like it was ready to explode. At that moment, I realized that I'd still thought that Jeff was exaggerating and that everything would be okay. Seeing him made me second guess my assumption. It was clearly underestimated. Now, I was worried.

Butch was unconscious, medicated with morphine and who knows what else. We talked to him like he could hear us, like we were back at the kitchen table talking about how great going into business together would be. I kept trying to make him laugh as if he'd been able to hear us. Hoping that maybe he could.

I don't pray. Not often, at least. For reasons that aren't important now, I did that day. Because when you see your partner in a situation like that, it's hard not to. It seems like the least you can do. The nurse gave us ten minutes and kicked us out. It was the last time I got to talk to him. He died three days after the accident. On the fifth. The odds were against him all along. Most people in his condition wouldn't have made it that long. The doctors couldn't get the swelling down and his internal organs started shutting down. One after the other, until his body just quit working.

I'd lost my dad to lung cancer that April. That hurt. Now, I'd lost my partner, best friend, and biggest supporter. It hurt more. Butch helped me germinate my entrepreneurial seed, the one planted in me on the curb in front of my parents' house when I was four. Together, we'd brought that to life and done well. Stuck with one another. He sacrificed a ton for me. For us. Including himself, ultimately. I owed him a lot. Maybe everything.

I delivered his eulogy. I couldn't believe that Dianne trusted me with that. It was hard to write and harder to deliver. The church was packed. I could see everyone from the altar. His family and friends. Coworkers and partners. I wondered what they were all thinking. Especially Rick, the hoarder who lent his hand to get us off the ground. He helped us get started and now look. His best friend was dead. I felt intimidated and responsible, like I had at Billy's funeral eight years earlier. There was an unmistakable pattern to that.

I did my best to let people know how special he was. What an honor it was to know him. How he changed my life and so many others. How much I would miss him. How much we all would.

Butch's death changed a lot for me. I was already breaking before he died. Mentally, especially. I was still optimistic on the outside, putting on a good face of rugged perseverance and can-definitely-handle-it grit. But I was struggling on the inside. Not with the business as much as with myself. Always thinking about my mistakes and inadequacies, plentiful as they were. I thought constantly about what a piece of shit I was. How clearly less-than I was compared to everyone around me. It was grinding me down to nothing when I was alone with my thoughts.

Without Butch, I thought I would break for sure. I got close before. To the edge I'd say, when I became a felon. He'd always been there for me. Without him, it felt like my shadow would be the only thing beside me. A dark reflection. Just me, alone with my thoughts. It wasn't true. I still had lots of support. I just wasn't seeing or appreciating any of it. I made everything about me, instead. I obsessed about how I felt like a loser or about how I deserved more than what I had been dealt, especially the last few years.

I was tired too. Really tired. Run-down tired. Ten years of having a pager 24/7 will do that. Clipped to my pants during the day and my underwear at night. Afraid I'd miss a page if it was on my nightstand. Early on, it gave me energy every time it buzzed because it meant there was a job to do or a problem to solve. It was my chance to be the hero. Now, it made me miserable. I wanted to throw the thing out the window. Or run over it with the SUV.

I was always on because I thought that I had to be. It was a self-imposed requirement. I designed it that way, on purpose and for me. I didn't know any better. It was an obvious problem, but I was so close to it that I couldn't see how it could be solved.

After Butch died, I fell off the edge and into a deep Valley of Uncertainty, infused with quicksand and self-pity. A place to think about retreating, where I could be okay feeling stuck and sorry for myself. It was my hideout that I'd sit in until someone came to my rescue. I wanted someone to tell me none of it was my fault and give me the answer to all my problems. To give me my due. What I was owed. What was that, exactly? Not sure. It didn't matter. I would just hang out until the answer came, by messenger or epiphany.

In my Valley, I was entitled to be broken. It was the place where my mind let me deserve and resent feeing that way at the same time. A safe place for dichotomy.

When we started our business, our goal was to survive. We accomplished that. We made money, built a great team, and had stuff like new houses and fancy pick-up trucks with naughty personalized license plates. But it came at a high price. A collection of fuckups, accidents, reputations, and lives. They overshadowed the good stuff even though there was plenty of that, too.

The business wasn't a startup anymore. It had changed, and I had not. It was growing up, and I wasn't. I still treated it like it was a baby, like it still needed me to be the parent to change its diaper, take it to school, and protect it from bullies. Instead of the parent to help it become what it could become. I made the fatal mistake. Making my world super small. Thinking it was all about me. Being selfish about what I thought was mine. Holding its future in my entitled little hands.

We've all heard the advice. Work on your business rather than in your business. I'd heard it too. Many times. Intellectually, I got it. The advice made perfect sense, for someone else. In my head, the business wouldn't work without me being in it. A hard-working part of the team was my identity. If I stepped away to work on it, it might just slip away from me and die. I couldn't even wrap my head around how to get started working on the business. How would I get started and what would I do? Scary thoughts.

Besides, what I was doing was working, wasn't it? I mean, not perfectly, but if you diverted your attention away from what happened to Butch and Billy, forgot about the indictment and conviction mess, overlooked the broken compass, put aside some weight gain and hair loss and pretended that the Valley of Uncertainty was a famous mountaintop instead, what I was doing was working out pretty well.

You can talk yourself into anything. As unhappy, worn out, and confused as I was, I could still convince myself that it was working—that I was working—and believe it. The only thing in the way was the truth. If this was working, what the hell does not working look like? The truth was that I was an entrepreneur bumping up against the limits of my abilities. As a result, the business was also bumping up against its limits. Still, I was unwilling to do the work that needed to be done. On myself first, so that I could then do what was needed for the business. I wanted everything to stay the same but get better. A different outcome from the same inputs. I wanted a future that I wasn't yet willing to sacrifice my past for.

PART III

BREAK

19

FOUR
FALLACIES

Entrepreneurs often find themselves in places they don't recognize or know what to do with. It comes with the territory. It's rare that smoothly laid-out plans stay that way for long. The world outside your dreams and business plans has a way of messing them up. This Valley thing wasn't an immediate revelation. Something that just clicked and made sense to me all of a sudden. I didn't wake up one morning, look in the mirror and say, yep, I'm in the damn Valley. It wasn't like that at all. I just knew that things were different. Felt different. That something was wrong. I felt a constant and unpleasant pain. Maybe I'd lost a step or two. My head wasn't in the right place, but I couldn't tell you where it was.

It would have been easy to blame what I was feeling on something or someone else. I tried that for a while. An attempt to drive the attention in the opposite direction of me. The world had been very unfair to me over the last few years. Conspiring against me, it seemed—or I pretended.

The fact is that I had no idea what was happening or why I was feeling the way I was. My mind had always been sharp enough— my will strong enough—to push through this kind of thinking. This was weakness, I thought. Pure and simple.

But it wasn't weakness at all. It was uncertainty. About who I was, where I was going and when I would get there. If I were even able to get there. I was trapped by what I thought people thought about me. The manifestation of years of punching above my weight. Winning rounds here and there but taking a beating along the way. Getting right back in the ring without creating room for recovery. I kept going until I felt like I was no longer able to answer the bell. The only punch I had left was to throw in the towel.

Being dumped into this Valley of Uncertainty felt miserable, but it was a lucky break. Continuing to motor on as I was would have had an inevitable end. Me, completely broken. Frustrated beyond repair. An asshole of the highest order. Reminiscing about the good old days, before I gave up on everything, including my future. Deeding my property to someone or something else instead of claiming it.

The lucky aspect of the Uncertainty Valley wasn't immediately clear. I was too deep inside it to see that at first. It felt like the opposite of luck. The change of perspective took a few years to realize. The result of gradual movement combined with pauses to think, search, and listen. Accepting rather than avoiding introspection and honesty. Truths that I'd blinded myself to. Investigating fallacies. Root causes. I began to see what was missing. My bad habits and unproductive thoughts. The shitty belief systems I was anchored to. My fear of failure. Lies I'd made up. The real reasons I ended up here.

Investigating my fallacies in the Valley led to a remarkable breakthrough. A change of view that might not have otherwise occurred. There were many of them. Too many to focus on at once. The list needed to be narrowed. To a manageable number. Four is where I ended up.

I believed that I could handle everything that came my way. That was my first fallacy. I thought that I could outwork every problem I faced, and I could do it on my own, like Butch could for a long time. Nine lives' worth. I thought that I was exceptional. Not in a conceited way, just a natural one. Like it was simply and singularly true. When I struggled, I buckled down. Convinced that I just needed more time. That there was always more time.

Asking for help was like cheating. What I got suspended for doing in Mr. Herbers's eleventh grade biology class. For collaborating with some buddies on a test when we thought he wasn't looking.

Doing my own work had been important to me. But I realized in my Valley that I hadn't put any boundaries on what my work was. I accepted whatever came my way. And here I was.

The second fallacy was that I was responsible for everything that was happening to me. Good, bad, or indifferent. That was a dangerous one. It was an impossible load to bear. Mistaken thinking that can make you miserable, like I was. Looking for unhealthy coping mechanisms. Or resigned to towel throwing.

I had completely mixed up being responsible with having the responsibility. I could only be responsible for myself. That was a big enough challenge. I had *responsibility* for everything that happened in the business, and I had to deal with that appropriately. There's a difference there that I'd been missing.

The way I was thinking about my future was a third fallacy I discovered in my Valley. It was looking to me to be a lot like my past. Why wouldn't it be? I didn't want that. I could still say the right things to everyone on our team. I was always an optimist with them. About our company's future and everything else. Inside, I was less of one. I questioned whether it was possible for my future to be different. How could I expect that when I had no control over it? When I was walking around this Valley, looking for someone to show me the way out.

The fourth fallacy was isolation. I'd become a wall builder over the years. A mason of sorts. Isolation was the package around the other three fallacies.

Bob Lange and his boys were real masons. They did all of our concrete and blockwork. I've never mortared anything. Not a single block with my own hands. But my mind operated its own block-wall printer. The walls it made were invisible to everyone but me. They were strong and kept growing. Taller and deeper.

I realized what had happened. I'd built tall, strong walls to insulate me from the outside world. Ironic. I'd been so fortunate to avoid prison after the indictment. Granted the gift of freedom. At the same time, I was building my own prison. A place where I could be scared and safe at the same time. A place where I could focus all my attention inside, and where I already knew everything. In the Valley, I realized that I was afraid to venture off the grounds and exist on the other side of my walls. It's no wonder I couldn't see what my future was, the walls obstructed my view in all directions.

On top of these four fallacies, my stay in the Valley made me think about peaking early. Was I on the verge of being Peter Principled as an entrepreneur? Washed up. A hack.

It had happened before. In little league. I was a star player—a pitcher and catcher. I had the arm and the bat, the ideal combination. A few years later, in high school, things had changed. I struggled for a spot on the team. Coach Dougherty had to hide me in the outfield. My arm strength had disappeared. If my bat had done the same, I may have had to play lacrosse instead.

I hated being in the Valley, but it did me a big favor. I finally had time to think about things. Identify and acknowledge some truths and limiting beliefs. Fallacies. It gave me great questions and few answers. Did I have the courage to go after them?

A TRUTH PUNCH

I needed a plan to deal with the fallacies that I discovered in the Valley. They were clearly holding me back. Making me miserable and keeping me stuck. I let them behave like magnets. Holding me in place. Without a plan, I might be stuck here for a long time.

It's hard to make progress before you admit the truth. You have to be able to say that you have a problem in the first place. Especially if that problem is the self-sabotage kind. Despite the clear evidence, I wasn't yet willing to admit that this was my problem. One that I was responsible for creating and had the responsibility to change, provided I wanted a life that inspired me once again. Did I want that? Of course I did. Who wouldn't? It's what I told myself.

The right question was easy to ask but hard to choose. Which one was it? Was I willing to change, or did I know how to change? Like my He-Man action figure from when I was a kid, I knew that I, too, had the power. I just didn't have the solution or the guts to ask for help.

Since I couldn't make a decision, right or wrong, I did what anyone who isn't ready or doesn't know how to fix something does. I punted. Figured it was something that I would get to later. When the time was right, and the planets better aligned. I kicked my problem can down the road.

I hate excuses, but I have to offer myself one here. Maybe it will resonate with you.

At least some of the reason that I was in the Valley wasn't my fault. Pressure, ego, and ambition led me there. Competition between my partner, Larry, and me. You've heard a few things about him already. He was a great partner. I've heard a lot of lousy-partner stories, and that was one I couldn't tell. Not about him.

We never talked about our competition. It was just something that was always there between us. In the room, on the phone, or in the car. However we happened to be together. Now that I think about it, maybe it wasn't competition at all. We weren't racing each other or betting big against each other. Maybe it was just ego. Positioning. A quest to feel superior. Better.

Anyway, this thing, whatever you call it, was weighing on me for a while—way before I thought I was broken or ended up in the Valley. Larry was a hard guy to keep up with. It was probably in the way that I chose to process it. I was smart, and he was smarter. I knew a lot and he knew more. I worked hard and he worked harder. He was hard-nosed, too. A serious player. A guy who fired his sister and sued his brother.

He was definitely in his office more than I was in mine. His family was convinced that he was a workaholic and tried the intervention approach once or twice. It didn't work.

On my way to the Valley, I kept thinking that Larry was the model I needed to be like. Emulating him was a goal. If I could convince myself that I compared to him, it was proof of my ability. Evidence of success.

Until I was in the Valley, it never occurred to me that he might not be the right model for me. The right farmer for my crop, like Butch was.

We kind of had it out with each other one Saturday morning, months before Butch passed away. It wasn't one of my finer moments. I don't remember what we started talking about, but he started getting on my nerves about whatever it was. He could be a bit of a dick when he wanted to be, and that's the vibe that was coming through my earpiece. I walked right into that trap and started whining about all of the wrong things. Vomiting up things that weren't issues and dumping them on him as if they were. Like why was I working so hard? Fairness. Making it all about me.

He pushed my bullshit back in my face. "You sound like a bitch," he said. That was new. It felt exactly like the time Don the Dick told me to fuck off. Larry had never shoved shit at me like that. It tasted horribly and pissed me off.

I thought about that exchange when I was in my Valley. Who knows why certain things pop up when they do? Point is, I now saw that he was right, and I was wrong.

I was wrong for thinking it was smart to model myself after him. He was an admirable model in a lot of ways, but he wasn't me, and I couldn't be him. I realized that I needed to create my own model. One that I had the pieces to put together. A model that I could shape into something that felt right to me. That would give me the confidence to move beyond the shit that had happened. Move past my past. Past truths over which I had no control and couldn't change.

Admitting that I needed my own model and couldn't change what was true seems like a silly little step. Duh! But for me, that silly little step was progress. A first step on my climb out of the Valley and toward a future that I was avoiding.

21

TAKING INVENTORY

Wrapping my head around the four fallacies along with the punch of truth Larry provided gave me a new bit of courage and confidence. To think about a different future. Realize that there was a way out. I could see a path forward. I was still in the Valley, but its hold on me was beginning to weaken. The small progress was creating some momentum. I felt different, a hint of freedom maybe, the kind you get when you start to abandon an illusion you'd been fixated on.

I had a job to do that I hadn't been doing well. I was supposed to make my company as successful as it could possibly be, which meant that I had to be as successful as I could possibly be.

Instead of doing that, I created a Valley and put myself in it. I waited there for someone to do my job for me. For something miraculous to happen. God to tell me that I was good enough. Shame on me.

But I still wasn't completely free. Sure, I was seeing new possibilities, editing my belief system, and accepting inevitable truths. Beginning to believe that I wasn't actually broken. Now what?

The next step was fuzzy. I wasn't sure what to do, but I knew that my model needed work. It was full of problems that I needed to work out. I started with things I could change, like my competition with Larry.

As an experiment, I sat down with my yellow legal pad and created an inventory that I called **My Problems**. It was just a list, really. Nearly unreadable because my handwriting was so sloppy. Of course, reading it wasn't the point. Acknowledging it was. I listed all the problems that I may or may not have been responsible for. Blame could no longer be on the table. It was a waste of time to debate that any longer. What I needed to accept was that I had the responsibility whether I was directly responsible or not. That's the job. If it was in my world, it was my responsibility. I had to accept it. Own it. Do something about it.

Taking this inventory could have backfired and had the opposite effect. Instead of giving me the beginnings of a roadmap forward, it could have just strengthened the walls I'd built around myself instead. Made them even higher, deeper, and stronger. If I'd done it another time, I may not have been receptive. I would have been scared instead of motivated. The Valley did me a favor that way. It made me tired of being in it. Encouraged me to find my way out. It gave me a safe place to wallow in the sludge of my thinking and kicked me out when it felt like I was ready. Like mama bird does to her babies. Fly.

Maybe I'd be able to solve some of my problems on my own and the rest with some help. Maybe they didn't all need to be solved. Certainly not all at once. If I solved a few, I'd build more confidence that I was on the right track. That I was making progress and feeling better about me and the work I needed to be doing. The work to return to feeling happy and getting back to doing my job.

If you could have made sense of my handwriting, it would have said this:

I need to get over being embarrassed about what I don't know. Do you ever feel like you're a phony? Like you don't belong where you are? I felt like that all the time. It was irrational, but it felt real. Everyone I met was smarter and more successful than I was. I was anxious around these people. My temperature would rise, and my face would flush. When I talked, which was rare, I would get bright red with embarrassment. I didn't think that I belonged, and this would make me want to get back into my mason-built walls as quickly as I could.

I need to make fewer decisions and more choices. Choices are proactive. Decisions aren't. They aren't synonyms. They don't mean the same thing. I make too many decisions I don't need to make. They make me feel good but breed dependence.

Asking for and accepting help is OK. I thought that I could figure everything out on my own. All it took was focus. I could be my own lawyer and accountant if I had to, despite having no training in either discipline. Why pay someone when I could figure it out on my own for free? What was I giving up while I spent this time doing work I wasn't built to do? Didn't matter, because figuring it out on my own was who I was and why I was valuable.

I need less noise in my life. I'd gotten sucked into watching the market and listening to talk radio. They were sucking ambition and curiosity from my brain. I thought that they cared about me and were making me smarter. I didn't see that they were using me. Trying to get me to be and think like them. All they had were opinions, and I was mistaking them for facts. My facts. They didn't matter, but I was accepting them into my life like they mattered a lot.

My perfect problem is a problem. I was a pile-on-the-desk guy. Piles everywhere. Full of things that I'd started but hadn't finished. I told myself that I was thinking about them, like I was a philosopher or something. The truth was that I didn't know how to finish them or shouldn't have started them in the first place. There was a finish coming, I'd tell myself. Then, I'd move the pile to a new spot to make me feel better.

I'm too comfortable with being comfortable, and that's making me uncomfortable. While Butch had built and moved into his dream house, we bought what we thought was ours, too. It was nice, nicer than anything I ever thought I'd live in. Butch had his new pick-up, and I was driving a Lexus. We were making ten times the salary we made ten years ago when we started the business; when we were hungry, and our work was meaningful. Butch was dead, but I was still comfortable. I liked it. My fear of loss had become greater than the excitement of gain.

The score isn't the only thing that's important. I kept score of everything. You either won or you lost in my book. Did you get a bonus and not say thank you? I tracked it. When people on my team said something stupid like, "There's plenty of business to go around," after we lost a deal, I would seethe and think that they were weak. Winning and losing aren't the only options.

I don't need to be in control. Everything rolled up to me, because I wanted to be in control. It didn't need to be that way. We had good, competent, and, in some cases, exceptional people. I just hadn't created a system that allowed them to flourish because I wasn't sure where that would leave me if they did.

I need to grow and learn. I'd forgotten who I wanted to become. I had no plan. No goals. My habits weren't challenging me. They were supporting me where I was. I was getting what I'd deserved. It just wasn't what I wanted. I've learned everything I can from the people I work with, and they've learned everything that I have to offer them. I was reading a lot of books, but you can't learn everything you need to know from a book. I was scared to get out around other people because I might feel stupid and inadequate.

The walls have to come down. The answers aren't inside my walls. If I want them, I need to suck it up and get out there. Stop being such a pussy. Grow a pair and get searching.

My past is filled with things that happened. It's not who I am unless I choose it to be. Is that my choice? What is my choice? I had to get clear about that. As if I didn't already worry enough about what other people thought about me, the felony conviction pushed that feeling into overdrive. I was convinced that everyone would see me as less than them. I cared about that, and it paralyzed me even though it didn't matter. It was always the elephant in the room. It came in with me, and I hoped that no one would notice or pay attention.

The bar doesn't always need to be high. Measure against an ideal. I ended up in the Valley for a lot of reasons and hadn't paid attention to one of the biggest ones. I was never happy. We made so much progress as a company and a team. I was always grateful and thankful to everyone. Except me. Nothing was ever good enough. I focused on what we missed instead of what we accomplished. What I missed. I always missed something. How could I miss that? I had trouble stopping to smell the roses or celebrating a win. I trained hard. Any good coach will tell you that you can't train hard all of the time.

Stop feeling entitled. I'd only been in business for ten years, but I thought that it and the world owed me something. That I was entitled to have things the way I want them, or the way I thought they should be. David Meltzer says it takes an entrepreneur seventeen and a half years to become an overnight success. I wish that I'd heard that back then. I was rushing things, but I thought that I was running behind.

Get selfish. Selfish is a bad word with negative connotations. I didn't want to be described by that word. Leaders and heroes aren't selfish, right? Maybe the good ones are. To lead, you have to know where you want to go. That takes focus and planning. It's easy to avoid and that's what I was doing. I wanted to be the good guy. The selfless leader. The entrepreneur whom everyone likes. Helpful and available. Open door and all that. Being selfless made me feel valuable. Busy, productive, and frustrated.

Frustrated? Yes.

Writing out my list helped me understand things in a way I hadn't before. It wasn't an easy exercise. I had to admit things that didn't feel good to admit. I also had to put a plan together that answered big questions. How would I make progress on all of these things? What was I capable of doing, and what would I need help doing? Did I really want this change, and was I willing to do the work?

Without knowing it, writing all of this down created the beginnings of a road map. It put my intentions out there. Opened me up to assistance. Laid down a path that I could follow and think about. I wasn't looking forward to the journey, but I knew that the time for it was now. It had to happen. Change was an inevitability. And when things have to happen, well, they have to happen.

PART IV

BREAKING OUT

22

MAKING CHOICES

Admitting that you need help is the first step toward finding it.
That's what they say. Some people make this admission easily.
Others, like me, don't. Writing down my problems—taking that
inventory—was my initial admission. I don't know how I thought
it would feel, if I thought about that at all. Now that it was in front
of me, it didn't matter what I thought. It demanded attention.

Now I had a decision to make. Or was it a choice?

Is a decision the same thing as a choice? The definitions are
similar, but what about the spirit? Decisions have a reactionary spirit. They are responses. Speed matters with decisions.
People are waiting.

Choices have a different spirit. They're curated and considered. Deliberate and thoughtful. Decisions need to be made while choices don't. Decisions can be important, but they can also be third-person and detached. Choices are voluntary and personal. The decisions you make are a way for others to judge you. The choices you make are how you judge yourself.

I'd been making decisions my whole life. Lots of them. But choices, how many of those had there been? I chose to marry Jamy, and I chose to partner with Butch. I apologized to the judge for the choices I'd made before he sentenced me. I guess you could argue that a decision is a type of choice. That every decision I'd made had been a choice between one thing or another. I don't think that's the way it is. There is a clear difference. Only semantics can blur the line.

I stared at my problems. What made me make these choices? If they were all the result of decisions that I'd made, what was stopping me from choosing to make different decisions? *Nothing*. Clearly. Except for me.

That thought felt like a revelation despite its simplicity. It wasn't profound because it was so clear. I hadn't felt like I was controlling much of anything when I broke and ended up in the Valley. I was missing what was right in front of me now. My inventory was the proof that I could control my choices. I'd just mistaken them as decisions because I was comfortable making those. They were my excuse for not making choices.

"My Problems" inventory wasn't organized in any order. I just started writing and it ended up where it did. Something had to jump to the front of the line. The first thing I would work on. Something I could at least start on my own.

Choice was that first thing. I wanted to get out of the Valley. Decisions got me there and choices would light the path I would follow to get out. I was nervous about it. I wondered if I had the strength or the will it would take to become what I could become. To do the job everyone needed me to do.

It would be hard work. My instincts and habits would require new coding. The 0s and 1s reordered. Butch taught me that the best way to tackle hard work is to start. "You may not beat it," he'd say, "but if you run away, it will always beat you."

Too many people run away. The hard work was just starting. It wouldn't happen overnight, and I had to accept that. Be patient with it. I studied my problem inventory and reminded myself over and over about the transformation that I wanted to make. The move from decision to choice. Going in this direction couldn't be nearly as hard as staying where I was. After all, that path led me to my breaking point and tried its best to keep me there. How could I do worse than that?

THE MESSENGER

Johnny V owned the best steak place in town. A table for two would set you back a few hundred bucks easy. A lot more if you got the good wine, Kobe beef, or the seafood tower appetizer that were part of the staff's upsell script. He was a local celebrity. Young, rich, single, and successful. That's the way it looked. Everyone knew who he was. A lot of people did whatever they could to get close to him or pretend that they were friends.

I didn't have the balls to introduce myself to him the few times that I'd been to his restaurant and seen him. An introvert thing. Why would he want someone like me bothering him? Other people didn't seem to ask themselves that question. They all wanted to shake his hand or give him a "Hey, Johnny!" from across the bar to impress the people they were with.

Johnny was the keynote speaker at a breakfast meeting hosted by the Chamber of Commerce. Joining the Chamber was my first venture outside my walls. His suit was well tailored. Hair gelled back, like Steve, the recycling guy and kick-back pro. It was early for him to be up. Restaurant nights bleed into early mornings. He made a joke about it, and everyone laughed because it felt like you had to. He talked about working in his uncle's place as a kid. That's how it all started. Bussing tables and washing dishes. Taking out the trash. Dumping the fryer oil in a grease barrel when it was French- or fish-fried out. He talked about how all that and more led him to today, where he owned high-end restaurants in major US cities.

Near the end of the talk, Johnny got really quiet. Like he had a secret he was embarrassed to share. He admitted to the group that he'd been overwhelmed by his success. By the growth and the failures. By what needed to be done and not knowing how to do it. He paused and looked down at his shoes, like he was getting up the courage to go on.

He had my attention because he was sounding like I was thinking.

When he looked up, a grin was on his face. A sheepish and shit-eating one. He told this story.

A friend of mine told me about a program he was in that could help me. He promised me that if I joined and did the work, in three years I would be making three times what I was making and have as much time off as I wanted. He said that I would have my freedom back. That being an entrepreneur would be fun again. Something I wanted more of rather than something I wanted to run away from. I thought he was full of shit. No way that could be possible. That doesn't even make sense.

He paused and looked down again.

But he was right. Being in that program transformed my life.

The program was called *The Strategic Coach*. I wrote down the name on a sheet of note paper from the table and stuffed it into my jacket pocket. Before he shared this, Johnny had been talking to the whole group. After he did, it was like I was the only one in the room. Like he was my messenger. Showing me the map I needed to get myself out of the Valley.

I signed up for Strategic Coach that morning, while the excitement was still hot and heavy. A few days later, I was interviewed, accepted, and billed. The fee was a big number. The most I'd ever paid to attend anything before was $500. Strategic Coach charged ten times that, and you had to pay for a whole year all at once. No installments or refunds. It was a big deterrent to backing out.

I didn't think twice about it. I was betting that it would be THE THING that helped me make the rest of my choices a reality. All because Johnny gave me the impression that it would. The convergence of a man in a Valley searching for a solution intersecting with a messenger holding open a new door.

I got to the Strategic Coach office early for my first session. It was near O'Hare airport, close to where Al worked at the salad dressing factory. I was nervous. Being outside my walls did that to me. I was also excited and quiet. Typical me. The people were nice, and the food was great. I pretended to read the *Wall Street Journal* I brought with me while I ate a bowl of granola with yogurt and hoped no one would talk to me. I was probably giving off an "I'm-a-dick" vibe, but I was just scared.

Teresa was our coach. Throughout the day, she'd lead us through thought exercises and then break us up into small groups to talk it through. You had to be proactive about finding a group. They weren't assigned. Each time, I felt like reading my paper again so that I could skip my turn to talk. I wanted my walls around me.

One was an activity summary. She told us to write down all the activities that we did at work. I was all over that and had to turn over my page to write on the back because I ran out of room. I noticed that other people at my table were struggling with things to write down. Obviously slackers, I thought. I felt superior. Like I was running a real company that required someone with my ability and work ethic.

When we finished, she had us rate every activity one of three ways. We loved doing it. We liked doing it. We hated doing it. Last we had to circle the top three things that we loved doing. Ones that always gave us energy. That we could do all day without frustration. Teresa told us that our mission would be to design our company so that we were ONLY doing those three things. I laughed to myself about the impossibility of that. She lost me there.

The "when-we-would-die" exercise was even sillier. It was called *The Lifetime Extender™*.[1] Teresa told us that Strategic Coach's founder, Dan Sullivan, had a plan to live to the age of 156. Impossible. I hear you. That's what I thought too. Jim Jones, Kool-Aid shit.

Teresa asked us to write down the age we were going to die. I was practical and wrote sixty-five. Without thinking. My dad died a few months after he turned sixty, a little over a year ago from the day of the training. He had cancer that started in his lungs and ended up everywhere. He knew that he was sick for

---

1 *The Lifetime Extender™* is a registered trademark owned by Strategic Coach.

a long time before he told me or my sisters about it. He'd sworn my mom to secrecy. He only came clean with us when he ran out of options. When hope was gone. The doctors suggested that he get into hospice care so that he could die at home. He quit smoking in his forties when he had some heart issues, but it must have been too late.

If I could live five years more than Dad had, that would be a win, right? That was longer than Butch lived, too. And Billy.

She asked us how we wanted to feel the day before we died. Everyone said that they wanted to be healthy and happy. Hmm...if that's true, and you could continue to feel happy and healthy up until the day you die, how much longer would you want to live? She shut up to let that question sit with us, giving us time to reconsider. The numbers across the workshop shot up in ways I thought were ridiculous and impractical. Over one hundred in a lot of cases. I raised my number to eighty. I didn't believe it, but I thought that I had to play along.

I was ready to take off early to beat the traffic. I thought that the exercises were silly. Unimpressed, if I had to use one word for the day. I hadn't met anyone like me, either. I figured there wouldn't be any waste guys but was hoping there would at least be someone else who got dirty for a living. Most of the people in the workshop were wealth advisors and insurance brokers. I felt like we didn't have a lot in common without giving it a chance.

I drove back to Milwaukee and wondered how any of the stuff we'd done today would help me triple my income and increase my time off like my messenger said it would. It didn't make sense to me. It seemed woo-woo. If they hadn't made me pay for all four workshops up front, I might not have gone back. That was a good hook. Smart marketing. Something else that I should pay attention to.

Ninety days later, I was back for my second Strategic Coach workshop. I still wasn't getting it. I resisted because I owned my old thinking and didn't want to trade it in. Not totally and not yet. It wasn't until the time of my eighth workshop, 720 days later, that things started to turn for me. I was finally committing. I was breaking through my old habits and developing new ones. Submitting. My mindset was shifting and expanding too. I was chipping away at the walls that the mason in me had built. Walking my way out of the Valley. Every few months, I could feel myself needing less protection from the walls I built. The uncertainty that produced them was slowly eroding.

I don't regret that it took me almost two years to submit. A lot had to come down before new stuff could go up. After all, what I'd been doing was successful to a point, before I broke and ended up in the Valley. I do think about what would have happened for me if I'd submitted sooner. The gaps I could have avoided. How much further I might be.

For example, from Day 1, Teresa was telling us to get assistants. It would be impossible, she said, for us to only focus on our top three things without one. The chatter in the room suggested that most of the people already had that box checked. Stories spread about how they couldn't imagine what life would be like without them.

I was telling myself different stories. I thought assistants were for wimps. Only lazy people or ones who get off on status symbols needed assistants. My status was that I didn't need that. I was looking at Mount Rushmore and seeing only rock. Not the incredible sculpture that hid inside those rocks. A perfect problem impediment.

My ego and my "competition" with my partner, Larry, prevented me from acknowledging that I would benefit from the help. Truth is that I had a different kind of status problem. It convinced me that I enjoyed the challenge of doing everything on my own. That my standards were so high I couldn't possibly count on anyone else to maintain them. The fact that I could handle it made me special. Deal with that. It had to be obvious to everyone, right?

I was also afraid of what I thought people might think about me having an assistant. Would they wonder what was wrong with me? Would they think I was some kind of prima donna? What about the cost? Was adding an assistant's salary justifiable when I was already getting my work done? It felt like I was increasing the cost of me.

It took a long time to turn me, but I finally bit the bullet and hired Robin as my assistant in 2005. I admit that waiting so long was a big mistake on my part. She'd been an executive assistant her whole career. She knew the drill and I knew nothing. It's not easy letting someone new into the intimacy of your work—into you. At least it wasn't for me. It took time for us to develop our system. Once we did, my life started improving dramatically and in ways I'd never anticipated.

Right off the bat, she helped me solve my perfect problem. I became more productive immediately. Take that silly activity summary I'd created in my first Coach workshop. I hadn't done much to change that in the past three years. I was just frustrated about it. But there were so many things on the list that had to go. I'd labeled so many tasks as ones I hated or only liked a little but kept doing anyway. These were the ones causing the grind, the wash-and-repeat cycle. What would I do if I didn't do those things? That was the question that having Robin helped me to finally answer.

I told her what I wanted, and she began taking away activities. Doing them herself or working with the rest of the team to find out who could do it for me. I didn't have the courage to do that. She wasn't burdened by that. She just did it. Working with Robin gave me a lesson in humility as well. As soon as my team found out that working through Robin would get them what they needed from me, they couldn't care less about what I was doing. That hurt me before it helped.

Robin freed my mind. Working with her gave me the permission to do my job. The job that I'd been avoiding doing. I did less. Sometimes I did nothing. Having less to do was liberating and a burden. I had more freedom but hadn't yet mastered what to do with it. Being productive took on a new meaning. I could no longer confuse being busy with being productive. Game escalation initiated.

What Teresa had been teaching me began to seem possible once I had Robin on board. What would I do if I only did the things I loved doing and that mattered most? How would I feel about that?

There was a reason those piles on my desk had been growing rather than shrinking. It wasn't that the piles represented things that weren't important. At least some of them were. They needed to get done by someone. On my desk, the piles were proof that I wasn't the right someone. Procrastination masquerading as the pursuit of perfection. They were things that I wanted (and we needed) but I didn't want to do. So, they sat in professorial-like piles undone and benefiting no one.

Robin made the piles disappear. She gave me the time to be creative and focus on the things in the business that needed my attention. Like me and the things that I should be doing to move the business forward. She got me back to doing my job.

I don't regret taking so long to finally hear Teresa's advice. Regret is a big waste of time, I was learning. Sure, I punted a couple of years of opportunity and time. And yes, while I was judging my workshop colleagues as lazy or status seeking, I was the one who was ignoring the forest for the trees. I only saw what was, or what I thought was. I wasn't thinking about what was possible. The future not visible in the present. I can't change who I was then, or the way I thought. The delay was just another toll I paid on the path out of the Valley.

THE FIVE WORDS

Sometimes a few words can change everything. In my case, it was five words. I knew the words. Everyone knows the words. You know the words. On their own, they are ordinary nouns, verbs, and prepositions. Together, in the right order, they are game changers.

Convergence happens when what you're searching for finds you. It can happen with a person, an idea, or an opportunity. You may not even know what you're looking for. You're unsure about it exactly. Still browsing through the racks. Sometimes it slams you in the face and other times it's so subtle you have to really be paying attention or you'll miss it.

I started slowly in Strategic Coach. Johnny V had said that it would be work, and I dragged my heels for a couple of years. That was also work, just the wrong kind. Eventually, I started submitting. Accepting what Teresa taught us in the workshops. Believing in it. The woo-woo made more sense to me each time. What I first found silly, I now embraced as profound. I gave in to the process, slowly and surely.

We received a binder for every workshop session. It had every-thing we needed for the day. The exercises and concepts we would learn or revisit. There were also three fluorescent-col-ored Sharpie markers, two or three CDs for us to listen to later in the car or on a Walkman. This was all before Steve Jobs made those disappear.

On each CD, Dan Sullivan talked about a concept we learned in the workshop. Or about something else that interested him. It was the one thing about Strategic Coach that I soaked up from the very beginning. I'd pop one in as soon as I started the car and get lost in what he was explaining on the way home.

Listening to Dan's CDs always expanded my thinking. As much or more than the workshop discussion. Sometimes, he just blew my mind. He told good stories. They were personal. They often started with something he experienced as a kid or as a young man. Growing up in the 1940s on a farm in Ohio or working as a reporter in the army during the Vietnam War. Sometimes they were about his college days at St. John's in Annapolis, Maryland. He pronounced it Mary-Land, and that always made me giggle, because most people I knew said it like Maralind, or just Marylin'.

The day that Dan changed everything for me with five words, he was talking about a school class reunion. His fiftieth grade-school reunion, I think. His classmates weren't looking at their lives the same way that he did, especially when it came to what was possible. He noticed that they saw their futures as uncertain and unpredictable, likely to be shaped by other people or things over whom or which they had no control. A force to which they were bound. A wind blowing the way it would blow. They were much more interested in talking about the past. It was known and certain, while the future was neither and scary.

Dan couldn't fathom approaching life like that. "*My future is my property*," he proclaimed. "It's not my mother's or father's. It's not my sister's, brother's, or classmate's. It's not my client's or my customer's. It's not the government's. It's mine. I own it. It's my property."

I wanted to pull over. This was my in-the-face convergence moment—a holy shit one.

Dan is a brilliant simplifier, and those five words changed everything for me. I'd been wandering around in my Valley, making progress slowly, like a baby shifting from crawling to standing. I was searching for the answer and here it was. My future is my property. I own it. It's not Butch's or Larry's. Not Billy's or my probation officer's. My competitors', no. It's no one's but mine.

Dan gave me the perfect opportunity to make a choice. If my future truly belongs to me, then I have to take its ownership. Making my future my property was a transformational concept. A thing that I had to do, a "how" that I had to solve.

I can imagine you thinking that it sounds simple or intuitive. Another *duh* moment for me. Or maybe you think it's crazy, that Dan is full of crap. Maybe you think I sound naïve for buying into it. No one can control the future. Whatever you're thinking, it's all fair. I was in that camp for a long time myself.

Here's the truth. The five words changed my life: my mindset, more precisely. Yes, I struggled with the "can't control the future" thing. That's an easy roadblock to throw up. What-about-this-or-that kind of thinking, I call it. An excuse to stop before you start. Why it won't work is always easier thinking than why it will. It's noise. I chose to accept that owning my future didn't mean I could control everything about it. That is impossible. I own my company, but I can't control everything that happens to it or in it. Same with my house and my car. Stuff breaks. Shit happens.

But no matter what, I've got a future to make my property. After I accepted that, "How?" became the question.

25

A NEW MODEL

Now that I was committed to making my future my property, I had to determine what that meant. The five words gave me the courage to choose to grow my company and me. I wanted to become the best entrepreneur that I could. To build the biggest company possible. What would that be? Ten percent bigger? Twice as big? Ten times?

Although I now had the courage, I still had a few bigger problems to overcome. Confidence was one. I was still struggling with being embarrassed about what I didn't know. That was holding me back. Making it hard for me to get myself into places where I could personally expand. Where I could feel like an imposter at first and be okay with it.

Models were another. Strategic Coach fine-tuned my mindset and exposed me to life-changing ideas and possibilities. What it didn't do was expose me to models that looked like the future I wanted.

The workshops were loaded with successful people running small companies. Teams of ten or less seemed to be the norm. Sales organizations mostly with lots of wealth advisors and insurance brokers.

I learned a lot from them. They had great business models. More attractive than mine, you could argue. They made a lot of money with very few moving parts and little capital expense. No trucks or heavy equipment. They didn't deal with safety departments or confined spaces. Their problems weren't my problems. We had a different set of obstacles on the road to making our futures our property. I was as unfamiliar in their world as they were in mine.

I needed to get involved with a different model and different people. A model with people who were once like me but had broken through the barrier I was up against. Grown beyond where I'd grown. I wanted to build a $50 million business and doubted that I'd get there if I didn't find a way to be around people who'd done that or more.

I'd heard about *The Executive Committee* (TEC)[2], many times before I decided to join. It wasn't a knee-jerk, Johnny V kind of decision. It was more of a logical, now's-the-right-time kind.

Getting outside of your comfort zone is a universal management-guru phrase these days. It's what people who want to be successful do, they say. Get comfortable being uncomfortable is how it goes. I agree with the advice. Sounds so easy, right?

Trouble is that there are forces working against the advice. Inertia and gravity for example. Making it easy to say but hard to do. At least that's the way it was for me. Intellectually easy and functionally difficult. I needed to break and spend a lot of time in my Valley, feeling comfortable and miserable in my walls, before I could begin to wrap my head around it.

In 2006, I faced the fear and took a chance on a new model.

Interviewing for TEC was uncomfortable. Its structure and orchestration were so not me. It was like a networking event

---

2 TEC is now a part of Vistage Worldwide.

where I was the guest of honor. Attention I did not welcome. It was a horrible place for me to be at the time. The meeting was facilitated by the group's chair. He led without being the leader. Stan was responsible for keeping the members in line and recruiting new ones.

I'd met with him once before and he explained the program. There would be a vetting process. I'd come to a meeting to be questioned and interviewed by the members. For an hour. Maybe more, maybe less, he said. They'd discuss and take a vote on whether I was a good fit.

I was forty. The youngest man in the room of all men by anywhere from five to twenty-five years.

The guys introduced themselves the way the chair asked. Name, company name, revenue, what you do, and years in TEC. Around the table they went.

Bob, ABC, Energy Controls, $120 million, twenty years.

Dennis, CDE, Publicly Traded Metals Technology, $500 million, ten years.

Dave, FGH, Restaurant Equipment—ESOP, $150 million, eight years.

It was obvious that I was in the right room. This was the company of the models I was looking for. Despite recognizing this was exactly what I was looking for, I couldn't help but feel a growing sense of imposter syndrome. It was different than what I felt with my Strategic Coach group. There, I was one of the bigger companies. I sometimes wondered how I could apply what we were learning in my kind of environment. Here, I was one of the smallest companies. I was worried how I could keep up or contribute.

The guys asked me a bunch of questions before I was dismissed. *Why do you want to join? How committed are you to growing? What are your blind spots? What kind of help are you looking for?*

When I joined Strategic Coach, everyone in the workshop with me was new, like I was. We had that in common at least. With TEC, it was a different story. It's never easy to join a group that's been together for a long time. Even if they're all warm and nice to you. It's hard to catch up. The group's got history and tribal knowledge you don't have. There are shared experiences and expressions, with an inherent nonverbal cadence as well. Making sense of it is a challenge. It takes time and attention. Patience.

Over time, I was sure that I would catch up. I told myself to just listen and wait it out. I took the two-ears-and-one-mouth approach. I couldn't expect to feel like an insider overnight. It was a tight club of people smarter and more successful than me. Exactly what I was looking for. Breaking in would take time. I just couldn't embarrass myself.

The typical TEC meeting structure is two parts. In the morning, a speaker gives a presentation on their area of expertise for about three hours. The topics span marketing, culture, leadership, and business process, for example. They were like a bunch of Dan Sullivans, sharing great stuff that made sense to me. Things I didn't know and hadn't thought about.

After lunch, we discussed what we learned from the speaker and what we intended to do with it. Sometimes it's a lot and others not so much. Then we moved to "issue processing." Here we helped each other with whatever problems we may be having. With our business, friends, spouse, or whatever. It's a time that invites vulnerability, where it's safe not to know. It has a "Board of Directors" feel to it. Except the TEC board can't fire you.

For the most part, I kept my mouth shut and my hand moving. I simply wanted to avoid sounding ignorant. I took notes on everything. I was in no hurry to be the smartest person in the room. I've seen others try that and it usually ends badly. They go back to where they can be that smartest person, with people they pay to be impressed. Or they end up all alone, maybe in their own Valley. I'd been there and didn't want to go back. There was plenty of time to inch my way into becoming a significant contributor to the group.

Roy Jablonka was my Johnny V in TEC. My messenger.

He ran a big company that made whiteboards and flexible packaging. A family business on the verge of transitioning to the third generation. To Roy's kids. He was planning his own exit.

Roy's hobby was digging holes and making roads. It was supported by serious yellow iron. Bulldozers, excavators, and loaders. His playground was his property up north. A place where boots, blue jeans, and flannel shirts were his uniform. Digging holes and making roads got him off. He kept the toys in his "shed" and made it sound like he and his wife slept on a dirt floor. The lingering smell of diesel exhaust providing the ambience. I think that was just part of his show. For effect. It romanticized his dream. I never saw the shed, but I have a feeling that Roy's shed was more like the lakefront mansion that a guy refers to as his cottage. Because that sounds humble.

Even though Roy had his future planned, he still came to the monthly TEC meetings to learn and stay sharp. He was a dichotomy. On the one hand, an aging businessman, steeped in tradition, gracious, and professional. A jacket, tie, and fedora guy. When he hosted meetings at his country club, he welcomed everyone at the door as they arrived, something no other member did. He made us all feel special, like he was on the Earth to serve us.

Then there was the Roy in the meetings. That Roy was a different story. One that got my attention.

Roy was never the smartest guy in the room. He knew that and embraced it. It never embarrassed him. Maybe it was because he'd been in the group for a few decades or maybe that was just how he was wired. How his brain chemistry was mixed.

During the presentation parts of meetings, Roy would fart, doze off, and ask crazy questions. That's what the rest of the group seemed to think. Most of his questions started with self-deprecation and ended with a kindly acknowledgment of the presenter's wisdom and knowledge.

"I might be the dumbest fuck in this room," he might start, rubbing his forehead with his hand and scrunching his face like he was in great physical pain. Then his question would meander through a story or two that would be difficult to follow. Finally, it would land at the speaker's feet. Once it was there, it would sit for a while. Like a bomb that no one knew how to disarm. The rest of the members would be smiling, giving each other a "That's Roy" look. The kind that you're all familiar with. Roy wasn't bothered one bit. He wasn't trying to be anything but him.

He waited patiently for the speaker's answer. If this was Roy's first question of the day, silence would usually follow its landing. A reset period while the speaker processed his dichotomy. They had to make sure they weren't missing anything. Because it's unusual for a well-dressed seventy-some-year-old man to start a question by calling himself a dumb fuck.

Because they were pros, their recovery almost always came quickly, and the best answer they could offer followed closely behind. No matter what answer Roy received, he pondered it with more head- and face-rubbing. "That makes a lot of fucking sense," he'd say. "You're so damn smart. I'm glad I asked. Thanks for being here."

Even though Roy had shocked the speaker with his dichotomy, he also made their day. Then, he'd doze off. All without any embarrassment.

Watching the Roy show take place month after month, I would have been the dumbest fuck in the room if the lessons he was dropping didn't make me think differently about my thinking. He didn't give a rat's ass about looking stupid. Instead, he embraced it. And here I was, always afraid of not saying the right thing, the smart thing. Choosing instead to say nothing. Being uncomfortable. Frightening myself. Turning bright red like I was being suffocated. Leaking sweat from my armpits.

Roy was definitely a different story. A story that I paid attention to. One that gave me confidence to accompany my courage. Emboldened by his example, I slowly broke through my fear and began to contribute more openly. Even when I was uncertain, I realized that I was the only one thinking the way I was thinking. No one else thought I was an imposter, unworthy, stupid, or whatever other lie I was telling myself.

It's unlikely that I'll ever be as Roy as Roy is, but he taught me to be as Mike as I can be. To be okay with what I don't know and with being wrong. That's just part of the journey. Comfortable being uncomfortable. Because those feelings are my opportunities to learn and improve. The reason I'm here. The job that I've chosen to do. The property that I own.

26

GETTING SELFISH

Jim Collins published *Good to Great* in 2001. I read it around then because everyone was reading it. Its title was intoxicating. It resonated. Who wouldn't want to know the secret to being great? I did. Its timing was great for me, too, as I was still thinking that I had a chance to do it. Become great, that is. It's a book about differences. About what happened differently at the great companies than at the good ones. The things that led the great companies to achieve stock price growth that the good companies could only dream about.

One of those was their assessment of the CEO. They identified the common attributes present in these CEOs and were surprised by what they found. Many were introverts. Comfortable being alone and operating backstage, away from the limelight. They were the heroes of stories that they didn't feel they needed to tell. They *"displayed a powerful mixture of personal humility and indomitable will."* The leaders had monster-size ambition, but it wasn't personal ambition. Not solely, for sure. The cause that mattered to them was the organization's, not their own. They knew their role and what they were there to do.

Collins called them Level 5 leaders and placed them at the top of the leadership pyramid, above the competent and effective leaders. He concluded that Level 5s "build enduring greatness," while the others essentially just get things done. Or make it all about them, like Al Dunlop or Lee Iacocca.

When I finished the book, I badly wanted to be a Level 5 leader. It felt like the perfect model for me. I had the will, that's for sure. And humility, too, most of the time. Where I fell short for sure was with the enduring greatness thing. We weren't even close to great at the time. That would have to come first. The enduring part was simply off the table. And my track record for greatness was really mixed as well. That record took another hit again in 2003 when Butch died.

The Level 5 thing sloshed around in my brain for years. It was still with me a couple of years later when I broke and fell into my Valley. Losing Butch put that on hiatus. It was alive but dormant, hibernating. It hadn't been fed in a while because it was planted very far from my front of mind.

Strategic Coach, TEC, and time had helped me put the Valley in my rearview mirror. The uncertainty that dropped me there was reducing as each new mile clicked by. They had me nearly back on flat ground, leveled. I could finally think about climbing again. The whirlwind that followed Butch's passing was calming. Fading, while never forgotten. My courage and confidence were growing. The walls were coming down a block at a time. I was under the influence of a new mindset. Being exposed to new ideas. The five words were making more and more sense. It was a grind, but a good one. Every day I walked further away from where I wanted to quit and closer toward something new, better, and maybe great.

Still, something was missing. I knew that I was on the right road, but I still seemed to be missing the mark. I felt like a running back who always wants to bounce the play outside when the huge hole is in the middle. A straight line is always the fastest way, and yet I was zigzagging. Was it a focus and discipline issue? Maybe fear. I needed a better system for hitting the right hole.

Months of searching narrowed down the problem. Direction. I'd been filling my mind with all kinds of new tools and concepts from Coach and TEC. Getting comfortable being uncomfortable. But I wasn't being deliberate about what I needed to do to put all that stuff into action. To hit the right hole. As a result, a lot of the ideas began to pile up. Big piles of half-baked stuff in my mind. Begging for my attention. The invisible version of the ones on my desk that Robin got rid of.

Collins made it seem like Level 5 leaders were servants to their company and its mission and not themselves. That Level 5-ers put every need ahead of their own. Serving others was what made them special. Taking a back seat was their superpower. So, that's what I did.

I missed the irony that that's what got me into trouble in the first place. Putting myself last and my pager first. Ignoring my Robin lesson. Making everyone's present my property instead of making my future mine.

I totally missed what had to be true for the Level 5 leaders. That deep down, in a place they loved but didn't want to talk about, Level 5 leaders were deeply and unapologetically self-ish. That had to be true, I figured. Without being selfish first, they couldn't have led their companies to achieve the results that great companies achieve. Without being selfish first, they wouldn't have known what that future needed to look like.

I don't know where that revelation came from exactly. Probably a by-product of what I was learning. Outside of my disappearing walls. All I knew was that I had to make another choice. A hard one. One that I fretted about for a long time. Thinking about it went against who I thought I was. The part that maintained a goodness about me. Without a new choice, it would be difficult to achieve the goal of making my future my property.

I had to get selfish.

Ugh. I know, it sounds horrible. But there was no other option. I had to get selfish with my ideas, with my time, with my focus, and with my attention. To know what I wanted my property to be, I had to design a structure in which I could operate selfishly.

It wasn't lost on me that *selfish* can be such an ugly word. People like Don the Dick are selfish. They have huge egos. They're also pricks and a whole lot of other negatives. Oh, and people hate selfish people. It's the last thing that I wanted to be known as. It went against everything I thought to be the "right" way. The selfless, servant-leader way. It was exactly the opposite of what Collins' book was saying about Level 5 leaders.

Although it's what I knew I needed to be, I was scared. I knew what I needed but I still cared about what other people thought. I wanted my selfish pursuit to be a positive thing for everyone. Like self-motivated or self-confident. Having great self-esteem. I hoped that I could pull off becoming more selfish without anyone else knowing.

I wanted my selfishness to be a good thing for everyone, not just me. At its core, being selfish was about freeing up time for me to think. To get clear about how I could make a bigger difference and become more valuable to my team and my company. To create a future that was our property.

There was no other way. I had to be operating at the top of my game. I had to know what I wanted. My thoughts, habits, health, influences, and relationships had to support the most optimal operation of me. I needed to be as fine-tuned as I could be. If I wasn't selfishly working on that, I knew I'd be doomed to sub-excellence. Or a perpetual stay in the Valley. That just wasn't an option.

It was a long and imperfect process. Not at all like flicking a switch. Becoming selfish was harder than I thought it would be. Some days it felt like I was going against gravity. I got used to it by taking small steps. The way you get used to most new things. Being selfish was helping me leave the Valley behind while taking ownership of my property. Slowly, I began to better understand my role as an entrepreneur. About how to lead the company at this stage.

I've remained devoutly selfish because it works. I know it sounds weird, but I'm proud of my selfishness. Without it, I wouldn't be where I am. I wouldn't have gained the understanding or the clearness of thought. About what it takes to create a future that was my property and build a team that could make that future a reality. A team with skillsets different than mine and more complementary. The necessary skillsets. I wouldn't have allowed mistakes to happen or failures to occur. I would have spent all my time trying to prevent those. Making prevention the lesson instead of failure the education. I would have missed the teaching moments. The progress and the reward.

27

ORDER

When Johnny V sold me on Strategic Coach that morning, I heard it like it was a magical formula. *Triple your income and multiply your free time*. He never said that it was magical. Or a hack to bypass the system. That was just what I thought I wanted to hear.

Turns out that Strategic Coach isn't about magic at all. Everything about it was work. A different kind of work. Work that I'd never done and didn't know how to do. In my Valley, I was wishing for something new and different to be delivered to me. From on high, maybe, or from the Universe, like the book *The Secret* promised.

Teresa didn't show me hacks. Instead, she taught me about systems.

Of course, I resisted at first. With good reason, I thought. I'm an entrepreneur and we hate systems. Right? They cramp our style. Systems are so *corporate*. We entrepreneurs are outlaws. Anti-corporate. Rule breakers, not system followers. We don't like to be told what to do. We color outside the lines. Our gut is our game. Ready-shoot-aim is how we play. It's how we win.

Over time, I came to understand the truth about systems. About how they make you better. And not just you. They make everyone on your team better. Systems make your company better. Like oxygen, they're required for you to live.

What Teresa and Strategic Coach taught me about systems made me think differently about the reasons why I'd broken and ended up in the Valley. I was thinking it was because of the decade of grind I'd put in and the adversity that came with that. Losing Billy and Butch, along with some of my freedom. Confusing responsibility with being responsible. All that. What I hadn't ever thought about was why the grind lasted as long as it did.

The grind was a sign. I understood what it felt like, but I missed why it was there in the first place. And why it had stuck around all these years.

The reason was me.

My business didn't create the grind. My clients and team members didn't either. It was me. I did it by designing my life to be a grind. Simple as that. It was the property I acquired.

When we were a startup, I craved grind. I loved it. It was how I kept my finger on the pulse. 24/7/365. It's what was needed.

Ten years later, I still craved grind. But now, I hated it. It was how I kept my finger on the pulse. 24/7/365. It's *not* what was needed.

I realized that systems weren't new to me. I'd always had them. My problem was that I'd created systems that required grind. A lot of entrepreneurs do that, I'm told. We want the grind to go away and forget that we asked for it in the first place. The grind was me getting what I'd asked for. The way I'd designed it to happen. Oops. My bad.

My resistance to systems started melting away. It was now clear to me that getting myself out of the Valley, making my future my property, and being able to be selfish would rely on me changing my systems.

Funny story about systems. Maybe you can relate. Osmosis was one of my old systems. I believed in it, but it never worked. I expected people to get it. To look at what I was doing, sense what I was thinking, and just do it. I asked everyone to model. Only I wasn't. Relying on osmosis was a grind producer. It was a shitty system. What was obvious to me wasn't to anyone else. How could it have been? My system frustrated me and confused them. That was dumb.

Every entrepreneur grinds. It's part of the game and unavoidable. Do too much grinding, though, and you eventually break or end up in the Valley. Questioning whether it's still worth it or whether you can hack it. In my case, I rode my own systems to that place. Maybe you're doing that, too.

When I understood what I'd done, it gave me the strength to know that I could change things. To reverse the course by modifying my systems. They had to support what I wanted—the selfish me. It was the choice I had to make. It would take work, just like it took work to create the systems that I'd had. I was motivated because I wanted to be able to say that I made Dan Sullivan's five words true for me. That my future was my property.

PLANS IN SAND

I could see that the light at the end of the Valley wasn't a train. The progress was clear. It was freedom. The light of day.

My messenger had arrived, and I was solving my perfect problem. Getting comfortable being uncomfortable. Roy's spirit perched on my shoulder. Dan's five words creating power inside me. I was becoming selfish, and my head was wrapped around the importance of systems. I was ready. Locked and loaded. Except for one thing.

I didn't know what I wanted to be when I grew up.

The only way for me to realize the power of my progress was to put it to work. I needed to be sure about what I wanted to be when I grew up. Without that, the progress would be wasted. I might end up right back where I started. In the Valley.

I'd spent the last couple of years focused on my problems. On fixing them. I knew what I didn't want and what I wanted to get away from. But where was I going? If my future was my property, how would I end up owning it?

People are always asking kids what they want to be when they grow up. They expect you to have an answer. "I don't know," doesn't cut it. Even when you hear, "That's OK" in return, no one truly believes that's an acceptable answer. You're supposed to know what you want to be when you grow up, no matter how young you are.

You don't get asked that question as much as an adult. Unless you're living in your parents' house too long without a job.

No one's usually asking an entrepreneur that question. At least no one was asking me. I wasn't even asking me. I was perfectly happy living a life of unaccountability. A well-deserved perk. Feeling like that's the least I was entitled to. Especially when I could blame the grind for breaking me and dumping my ass into the Valley.

When Dan Sullivan told me that *my future is my property*, I should have known that there would be a lot more to it. More work, like everything in Strategic Coach—and in life. Because the property would be mine, I had to know what I wanted it to look like. I needed a picture that I could visualize and explain. That was the first step. But that alone wouldn't be enough. I also had to know how to get there. Or at least how to get started knowing how to get there.

I'd gotten better at beating back or ignoring my perfect problem. But it never went away. It was always hanging around. Competing for my attention. Still is. When I thought about my future property, I wanted a perfect answer. I looked for a crystal-clear plan about how to get there and what it would look like. I wanted to know the one step that would get me from here to there.

My perfect problem had been wrong before. Many times. And it was wrong again about this. Maybe wrong isn't right. Maybe it was more like it just didn't understand. My perfect problem was just an excuse-maker. If gave me an out any time I couldn't see the straight line from here to there. Just wait for the path to reveal itself, it would tell me. Hang tight. Relax. You don't want to make a mistake.

That wasn't going to work. The ton of progress I'd already made on my way out of the Valley was at my back. Pushing on me hard, like a lineman on the pile to get the running back over the goal line. It was going to move me no matter what. I just needed to give it some direction, to tell it what I wanted to be when I grew up.

I used to have goals, but I kept them to myself. Only I knew about them. I could grade my progress on my own curve. Whether I accomplished them or not, nobody knew. Except me, and I wasn't talking. Goals were complicated for me. By this time, I'd been goal-less for some time. Years. I was letting life happen to me. Showing up to see what would happen. Taking what it gave me. You know where that led me.

Chuck Zamora is a smart friend of mine and a teacher. He educates on life and is big on quotes. He sent me an email, like he knew I was struggling. It had a picture of an ocean wave breaking on the beach behind the words "goals in concrete, plans in sand."

Everything clicked for me after reading that. I hadn't been struggling with the goal. It was the plan. My perfect problem wanted a perfect plan. I didn't have that. That's what was keeping me stuck.

Chuck's email gave me the permission I'd been denying myself. Permission to establish goals about the things I wanted. Even if I had no idea how to achieve the goal. No more. It was now satisfied.

The reality was that my future was a product of my imagination. It let me want whatever I wanted. It didn't expect me to know how to get to it. It just wanted me to get going.

Chuck got me going. I learned quickly that the great thing about a setting a goal is that you always make progress toward it. Every inch of progress is a new sprout of capability. Whether that progress leads to achieving the goal or not, my confidence and courage grows. I always get bigger. It's okay if I end up on the wrong path or going in the wrong direction. That's not a waste of time. It's not disappointing. Realizing that I took a step in the wrong direction is the first step toward going in the right direction. Goals in concrete. Plans in sand.

Once I understood how to make goals work for me, they became the bow on top of my *get-and-stay-out-of-the-Valley* present. I was all in. Goals made me intentional. Working toward them forced me to structure my thinking. To break the goal down into manageable bites. Small steps that could lead in the right or wrong direction without much consequence. Doing it this way melted away my perfect problem because it removed the fear. It was hard to get hurt or look stupid.

I shared my goals with my team and others that could help me achieve them. I wasn't afraid anymore to ask for help. That didn't make me feel weak or lazy like it used to. Instead, it made me feel powerful, capable, and entitled.

29

ERASER DUST

When I was a student at St. Denis School, we took turns clapping the erasers at the end of the day. It was fun to get chosen by our teacher to do it. We made it into a contest to see who could make the biggest cloud of dust. Or how much chalk we could clap onto each other's uniform. The erasers had collected the day's lessons from the classroom blackboards, and we were making space for new ones the next day. We liberated the lessons with our clapping, and they flew into the afternoon air. Each was carried away before eventually landing somewhere else. Erased but not forgotten. None of us thought much about what was happening. Or whether it was smart to breathe that stuff. We were just grade school kids. Doing a job that our teacher assigned us.

I forgot about eraser clapping for a long time. Along with what it represented. While I was operating inside the walls I'd built, I wasn't erasing anything. My chalkboards were filling up with information I already knew well. Or wanted to forget but was fixated on. Constant reminders of a life that was different than what I wanted. Of inadequacy and failure. Ignoring all the good. A giant obstacle that couldn't be avoided.

When the grind dropped me into the Uncertainty Valley, I expected someone to come along and fix things for me. To erase the blackboards of my own decisions and give me a new story. One that made me look better and showed me the way forward. Or give me permission to give up. Make it okay. Get a do-over. Make fixing my life someone else's problem and responsibility. Blow out the excess inventory. At fire-sale prices, if necessary.

If only life worked like that for entrepreneurs and everyone else. Thankfully, it doesn't. No matter how much you sometimes wish it would. It doesn't because all our limiting beliefs—the ones we try to erase or pack away in that part of the basement no one ever looks in—are created, designed, and controlled by one person. In my case, that's me. In yours, it's probably you.

I wrote my story and decided what it meant. The walls I built felt real. They weren't. I created them. Out of thin air. Then, I decided that they were real. The same happened with my Valley of Uncertainty. It was a made-up place that I wanted to be real because I thought being there would give me an out, an excuse for why I wasn't who I knew I could be.

There's no such thing as a good or bad story. Stories just are. They're things. Products of choices. Some I like talking about openly. They're safe. Others I only talk about with myself. Because I don't like the way they sound. Especially out loud, in public spaces. Processed through others' ears.

We decide what our stories mean. I wish I'd figured that out earlier. That I'd read a book about it or attended a seminar that explained how our stories impact us and the people around us. We can change what we decide our stories are or stick with them forever as we first imagined them. There's a chance for danger and uneasiness no matter how we choose. There's an equal chance of opportunity and progress.

I got stuck in stories that I should have erased. I should have turned those into dust. Wiped them off the blackboard, for my own protection. My psyche might be better off if they'd never happened or couldn't be Googled. But they're all I have. My property. Erasing them didn't mean they'd be forgotten. You can't undo what's been done. Erasing is more about creating space. Making room for new parts of your story to be added. Similar to what happens when you create a new habit. Your new habit replaces one that no longer serves you the way you want. You don't forget your old behaviors. You just don't use them anymore—at least not in the same way. You make different choices based on new information and goals. The result of making my world a bigger place with more space was a new frontier. I had the freedom to write my story with a new mindset and a fresh approach.

I wish my messenger had found me before I made the choice to break. Or that someone would have been there to punch me in the face. Alter my perspective. Talk sense to me. Throw some cold water on me. Remind me to erase.

Where would I be today if only I'd been open to that sooner? When you don't know what you want, you often get what comes your way.

I had a bigger story to tell and a bigger, more successful company to create. The same is true for you. Entrepreneurs are some of the most special people in the world. Powerful, optimistic thinkers. Delusional, yes. But also caring, hardworking, and fearless. Even when we're afraid, we deserve to make the maximum impact possible on the greatest number of people. And have a responsibility to use our unique talents to build people and companies. To make our future our property and achieve dreams. Big ones.

Think big. Find help. Design your future and claim it as your property. Enjoy!

ABOUT
THE AUTHOR

Mike Malatesta started his first business in 1992, seven months after being fired from a company he had dreamed he might lead one day. Over the next twenty-two years, he helped run, lead, and grow that startup, selling it for more money than he could have imagined.

The creator of the *How'd It Happen* podcast, Mike is deep into his second startup and an active early-stage investor. His mission is to help as many entrepreneurs as he can to create companies that improve people's lives and, maybe, the world.

Mike lives in Wisconsin with his wife, Jamy. He's active in YPO, Abundance 360, and Vistage International. Connect with him online at mikemalatesta.com.

CPSIA information can be obtained
at www.ICGtesting.com
Printed in the USA
BVHW080314161221
624012BV00011B/654/J